True Reformers

Saints of the Catholic Reformation

STUDY GUIDE

Dr. Christopher Blum

Copyright © 2017 Augustine Institute. All rights reserved.

With the exception of short excerpts used in articles and critical reviews, no part of this work may be reproduced, transmitted, or stored in any form whatsoever, printed or electronic, without the prior permission of the publisher.

Some Scripture verses contained herein are from the New Testament, copyright 1946; Old Testament, copyright 1952; The Apocrypha, copyright 1957; Revised Standard Version Bible, Catholic Edition, copyright © 1965, 1966, Division of Christian Education of the National Council of the Churches of Christ in the United States of America; Revised Standard Version Bible, Ignatius Edition, copyright © 2006, Division of Christian Education of the National Council of the Churches of Christ in the United States of America.

English translation of the *Catechism of the Catholic Church* for the United States of America, copyright ©1994, United States Catholic Conference, Inc.—Libreria Editrice Vaticana. English translation of the Catechism of the Catholic Church: Modifications from the Editio Typica copyright ©1997, United States Catholic Conference, Inc.—Libreria Editrice Vaticana.

Writers: Sean Dalton, Julia DeLapp

Print Production/Graphic Design: Jeff Cole, Brenda Kraft, Devin Schadt, Christina Gray, Ann Diaz

Media: Steve Flanigan, Aurora Cerulli, Jon Ervin, Matthew Krekeler, Justin Leddick, Kevin Mallory, Ted Mast, Molly Sweeney

Augustine Institute
6160 South Syracuse Way, Suite 310
Greenwood Village, CO 80111
Information: (866) 767-3155
Augustineinstitute.org/programs

Printed in the United States of America
ISBN 978-0-9982041-7-8

TABLE OF CONTENTS

An Introduction — 4

Session 1: Saint Thomas More: The Age of the Author — 9

Session 2: Saint Ignatius of Loyola: Soldier for Christ — 17

Session 3: Saint Philip Neri: The Apostle of Joy — 25

Session 4: Saint Charles Borromeo: The Good Shepherd — 33

Session 5: Saint Teresa of Ávila: A Study in Perseverance — 41

Session 6: Saint Francis de Sales: Pastor of Souls — 49

Suggested Answers for Group Leaders — 57

True Reformers

SAINTS OF THE CATHOLIC REFORMATION

AN INTRODUCTION

Welcome to *True Reformers: Saints of the Catholic Reformation*, a study crafted to teach about those who led the Church's rebirth from the ashes of confusion caused by the Protestant Reformation. In these six sessions, participants will learn about the true benefactors of the human race: the saints. The saints of the Catholic Reformation show us just how powerful—and beautiful—is the human heart's free response to God's generous grace.

HOW THE STUDY WORKS

This study is composed of the following sessions:

1. **SAINT THOMAS MORE: THE AGE OF THE AUTHOR**

   The Renaissance was an age of discovery and innovation during which many lost their way amidst bold new visions of secular happiness. Thomas More was one of the greatest humanists of his age, but also a man devoted to the spiritual life. His lifetime of learning, charity, and service to the public good of England enabled him to stand a patient and holy witness—and one of the greatest of modern martyrs—against the tyranny of Henry VIII.

2. **SAINT IGNATIUS OF LOYOLA: SOLDIER FOR CHRIST**

   While Martin Luther's interior troubles plunged Europe into a maelstrom of controversy, confusion, and war, the Basque soldier Ignacio de Loyola set out on an extraordinary interior pilgrimage of grace. Taught directly by God, Ignatius offered the Church a new spirituality of devoted service to Christ and founded a religious order dedicated to evangelization, the Jesuits.

3. **SAINT PHILIP NERI: THE APOSTLE OF JOY**

   To a Rome ravaged by war and wearied by the decadence of the Renaissance popes, Saint Philip Neri came as an unlikely reformer. Mystic, hermit, prankster, and effortless leader of men, Neri had a great sense of humor and an even greater heart. His creative response to the challenge of the Reformation era made him the Apostle of Rome.

4. **SAINT CHARLES BORROMEO: THE GOOD SHEPHERD**

   As the Cardinal-nephew of Pope Pius IV, Saint Charles Borromeo was one of the wealthiest and most powerful men in all of Rome. Yet he chose the extraordinary challenge of reforming the enormous archdiocese of Milan to the pampered life of a Renaissance prince, and willingly spent himself in the service of his flock.

5. **SAINT TERESA OF ÁVILA: A STUDY IN PERSEVERANCE**

   Nobly-born, wealthy, captivating, and headstrong, Teresa de Ahumada was unlikely timber for a great work of renovation. After many years of complacent living in a fashionable convent, Teresa was drawn into a mystical embrace and learned directly from Divine Inspiration what a life more pleasing to God would be. She spent the last twenty years of her life in a whirlwind of activity as the founder of the Discalced or reformed branch of the Carmelites in Spain.

6. **SAINT FRANCIS DE SALES: PASTOR OF SOULS**

   Determined from his youth to pursue the priesthood, Saint Francis de Sales lived a storied life as a priest and missionary before settling down to the duties of a small-town bishop in the foothills of the French Alps. The spiritual writings of this beloved teacher of everyday holiness are justly celebrated. In his doctrine, we find the summation of the teaching of the Catholic Reformation.

TRUE REFORMERS can be completed over the course of six separate meetings or during a day-long seminar.

LEADING A TRUE REFORMERS SESSION

THE STUDY GUIDE

This guide will take you through a step-by-step process for each session. Each section has been carefully crafted to equip you for self-study or to lead a group through an exploration of the saints of the Reformation. If you are a facilitator of a group, we have included suggested answers to help guide group discussions.

WHAT YOU'LL FIND IN EACH SESSION

OPENING PRAYER: Each opening prayer is drawn from the writings of the saints. Choose one person to read the prayer aloud; give others the option to join in or read along silently.

INTRODUCTION: Read aloud the Introduction to provide a brief overview of the session.

CONNECT Questions: Engage in conversation through two or three questions designed to help you start thinking and talking about what you'll learn from each saint.

VIDEO: Together watch an engaging video segment that teaches about the life of each saint. An outline of each video is provided. You'll also find space for note-taking at the end of each session.

DISCUSS: Each video segment is followed by questions to lead you through a small group discussion on the video teaching; suggested answers are included in the back this guide.

COMMIT: Use this prompt as encouragement to put what you've learned into practice in your daily life. Preview this as a group, and invite reflections on the activity next time you meet.

CLOSING PRAYER: The Closing Prayer has also been drawn from the writings of the saints. Again, choose someone to read the prayer aloud while others join in or follow along silently.

FOR FURTHER READING: Each session concludes with suggested resources for continued study and reflection.

HOW TO LEAD SMALL GROUPS

The success of any small group begins with an engaged leader. Leading a small group discussion does not mean you must lecture or teach. A successful small group leader facilitates, getting participants to interact as they make new discoveries. Here are some tips to help you get started as you lead and facilitate your small group:

- **SET THE TONE:** Let group members know from the beginning that your time together is meant to be for discussion and discovery, not lecture. Also remind your group that every question and answer is welcomed and worthy of discussion.

- **ENCOURAGE INVOLVEMENT:** Work to invite everyone in your group to engage in discussion. Don't be afraid of periods of silence, especially during the first part of the meeting. If one person gets off track, kindly acknowledge the person and invite him or her to explore that topic more after your group time. Ask questions such as "What do the rest of you think?" or "Anyone else?" to encourage several people to respond.

- **ASK OPEN-ENDED QUESTIONS:** Use questions that invite thought-provoking answers rather than "yes" or "no," "true" or "false," or a one-word, fill-in-the-blank answer. As a leader, your job is to get participants to think about the topic and how the lives of the saints can be relevant and applicable to their own life of faith.

- **AFFIRM ANSWERS:** People are often reluctant to speak up for fear of saying something wrong or giving an incorrect answer. Affirm everyone by saying things such as "Great idea," "I hadn't thought of that before," or "That's an insightful response." These types of phrases communicate that you value everyone's comments and opinions.

- **AVOID ADVICE:** Remember, you're acting as a facilitator—not a college professor or counselor. Instead of giving advice or lecturing, when appropriate, offer how a Scripture passage or something in the video spoke to you personally, or give an example of how you've been able to apply a specific concept in your own life.

- **BE FLEXIBLE AND REAL:** Sometimes your group time may veer off-track due to something that's going on in our culture or your community. Use relevant topics as a time to remind them that God is always with us and that in every situation we can seek guidance the lives of saints as well as from Scripture, the Church's teachings, and the Holy Spirit. If you model relevant discussion and transparency, your group is more likely to do the same.

- **STICK AROUND AFTER THE MEETING:** As the leader, make yourself available after your meeting time for questions, concerns, or further discussion on a topic that a group member may have been hesitant about during the scheduled time. If a question arises that has you stumped, admit that you don't have the answer and offer to contact someone who may be able to provide one, such as your parish priest or deacon, or your diocese.

MEETING OPTIONS

Below is the suggested outline for an individual session when using TRUE REFORMERS *over six separate 60-minute meetings.*

TIME	STEPS	OVERVIEW
10 Minutes	OPENING PRAYER/ CONNECT	Welcome everyone, share the Opening Prayer, and ask the Connect questions to get participants acquainted with the topic.
35-45 Minutes	VIDEO	Watch the video segment together.
10 Minutes	DISCUSS	Facilitate discussion of the questions in small groups.
5 Minutes	COMMIT/ CLOSING PRAYER	Lead participants on a brief overview of the Commit take-home assignment, end with the Closing Prayer.

Below is the suggested outline for an individual session when using TRUE REFORMERS *over six separate 90-minute meetings.*

Use the time allotments as a guideline; the length of time spent on each section will vary from group to group.

TIME	STEPS	OVERVIEW
5 Minutes	OPENING PRAYER/ INTRODUCTION	Welcome everyone, share the Opening Prayer, and then go through the Introduction of the session.
10 Minutes	CONNECT	Ask the Connect questions to get participants acquainted with the topic.
35-45 Minutes	VIDEO	Watch the video segment together.
20 Minutes	DISCUSS	Facilitate discussion of the questions in small groups.
10 Minutes	COMMIT	Lead participants on a brief overview of the Commit take-home assignment.
5 Minutes	CLOSING PRAYER	End with the Closing Prayer.

DAY-LONG OPTION

True Reformers can also be facilitated in a day-long program with shorter sessions. Here's an example of how you might structure the day:

> 8:00 a.m. Registration/Gathering/Introductions
>
> 8:15–9:15 a.m. Session 1
>
> BREAK
>
> 9:30–10:30 a.m. Session 2
>
> BREAK
>
> 10:45 a.m.–11:45 p.m. Session 3
>
> LUNCH
>
> 12:30–1:30 p.m. Session 4
>
> BREAK
>
> 1:45–2:45 p.m. Session 5
>
> BREAK
>
> 3:00—4:00 Session 6

SESSION 1
SAINT THOMAS MORE
The Age of the Author

Sir Thomas More's Farewell to his Daughter by E. M. Ward
© Restored Traditions. Used with permission.

SESSION 1
SAINT THOMAS MORE

OPENING PRAYER

Lord, grant me a holy heart that sees always
what is fine and pure and is not frightened
at the sight of sin but creates order wherever it goes.
Grant me a heart that knows nothing of boredom, weeping, or sighing.
Let me not be too concerned with the bothersome thing I call myself.
Lord, give me a sense of humor,
and I will find happiness in life and profit for others.
—Saint Thomas More

Connect

1. It's a common saying that the end justifies the means. What is the problem with this way of thinking and acting?

   _____
   _____

2. The Church teaches that each of us has a responsibility to contribute to the common good of society. How can we as individuals contribute to the public good?

   _____
   _____

> *"To believe in Jesus is to accept what he says, even when it runs contrary to what others are saying. It means rejecting the lure of sin, however attractive it may be, in order to set out on the difficult path of the Gospel virtues."*
> —Pope Saint John Paul II

Introduction

The Renaissance was an age of discovery and innovation during which many lost their way amidst bold new visions of secular happiness. Thomas More was one of the greatest humanists of his age but also a man devoted to the spiritual life. His lifetime of learning, charity, and service to the public good of England enabled him to stand a patient and holy witness—and one of the greatest of modern martyrs—against the tyranny of Henry VIII. In this session, we will look into the ideas and example of Saint Thomas More and learn how faith and virtue impact man's relation to politics, society, and God.

Video

The following is a brief outline of the topics covered in this 45-minute video teaching.

I. **St. Thomas More's Early Life**
   A. Grew up in the "age of the laity"
   B. Well-educated as a youth and served as page of Cardinal Morton
   C. Went on to study at Oxford and was influenced by the humanists
   D. Spent four years with the Carthusians
   E. Enjoyed a vigorous legal career
      1. Quickly rose in importance in this field
      2. 1529 named Lord Chancellor of England

II. **More's Self-Portrait:** *Utopia*
   A. Shows his wit and seriousness
   B. Subtly addressing the court
   C. Proclaims the truth and a new philosophy
   D. Commentary on the impracticality of socialism
      1. Utopians devoid of courage and chivalry
      2. Lack of respect for the dignity of human life
   E. Main purpose: ask questions critical to men and women
      1. What is truly good?
      2. What kind of life should be lived?

III. **The Corruption of Christian Ethics**
   A. Niccolo Machiavelli—focused on end, not means
   B. Martin Luther
      1. Invented new theology: we are saved by grace alone
      2. There is nothing to be done in order to become virtuous
   C. More's Response
      1. What directs our will: virtue is where our happiness lies
      2. Goods of the soul outweigh external goods

IV. **The Noble Deed of St. Thomas**
   A. Divorce of Henry VIII—knowledgeable king acting against his conscience
   B. More resigned his position as Lord Chancellor
   C. Henry VIII attempts to change More's mind
   D. St. Thomas sent to Tower of London
   E. Dying words: "I die the King's good servant, but God's first"
      1. Served the king by serving the law, common good, and truth
      2. Witness of truth—devotion to God above all

Discuss

1. Saint Thomas More was a man of integrity. He refused to take the Oath of Supremacy by which he would have sworn allegiance to the King of England as the supreme governor of the Church. Consequently, he was convicted of treason and beheaded. Saint Thomas More would not compromise his Catholic Faith.

How would you respond to someone who says that the Church will become more relevant in society if she de-emphasizes, or even changes, those teachings that conflict with secular progressive values?

_____
_____
_____
_____

2. The saints are great models for us! Their lives demonstrate what is possible when one's will more fully cooperates with the grace God freely offers. In addition to their example, Dr. Blum says the saints can also be great friends to us.

How could you help an Evangelical Protestant understand the role of the saints in our lives when they believe that the Bible strictly forbids any form of communication with the dead?

_____
_____
_____
_____

3. Dr. Blum says that "the human soul is where God spends all of his efforts." In other words, we are the crown of his creation and our sanctification and final glorification is the intended purpose of our existence. Bottom line, God wants us to be saints. The only obstacle to his efforts is our own unwillingness to become saints. Saint Thomas More addresses this drama in *Utopia,* as the Utopians are not necessarily living with the end in mind. Truth, goodness, and courage are the necessary ideals for living with the end in mind.

If you were to develop a personal mission statement aimed at becoming the person God desires you to be, what would be your goals and your plan to reach them?

_____
_____
_____
_____

4. Martin Luther believed that human beings are not truly free. In his work *Bondage of the Will*, Luther argued that our will is either controlled by God or by the devil. It is for this reason that he taught that salvation is obtained by grace alone and faith alone. Saint Thomas More wrote this about Martin Luther's theology: "That everything depends only upon destiny, and that the liberty of the human will serves absolutely no purpose, nor do people's deeds, good or bad, make any difference before God … [is] the very worst and most harmful heresy that ever was thought up; and, on top of that, the most insane" [Saint Thomas More, *Dialogue Concerning Heresies* (New York: Scepter Press, 2006), §11, p. 453].

Why would Saint Thomas More consider Luther's teaching on human freedom and salvation "the very worst and most harmful heresy that was ever thought up"?

_____

_____

_____

5. In the fictional work *Utopia*, the character Hythloday tries to convince Thomas More that Utopia is the most perfect of societies. He says, "In Utopia, where there is no private property, everyone is seriously concerned with pursuing the public welfare." As such, the moral education of the young in Utopia is aimed at their eventual contribution to the public welfare of the state. Hythloday's cynical view of the human person, who he considers to be prideful and greedy, thinks him incapable of private ownership and the building of a just society. However, Thomas More is not convinced.

With the Catholic Church's commitment to justice and the common good, why does the Church oppose those forms of socialism that seek to abolish the private ownership of property?

_____

_____

_____

6. Saint Thomas More's family was always his first concern. Their home was full of love and security. He was personally invested in developing the minds and faith of his children. His close friend Erasmus, who made lengthy visits to the More residence, said: "I should rather call his house a School of Christianity for while there is no one in it who does not study the liberal sciences, the special care of all is piety and virtue. No quarreling or ill-tempered words are even heard and idleness is never seen."

A host of reputable studies demonstrate that a father is essential to the healthy development and total well-being of his children. And yet, from pop culture to the media, it would seem our nation places little value on the role of fathers. Why do you think this is the case, and what can be done to empower fathers?

_____

_____

_____

Commit

In the words of Erasmus, Saint Thomas More's house was a "School of Christianity." Our commitment this week is to study the Faith with our families. One suggestion is to watch an episode from a video study on formed.org and have a discussion. Even if your children are raised and out of the home, invite them to watch the same episode and have a conversation to follow up.

"Render to Caesar the things that are Caesar's, and to God the things that are God's."
—Luke 20:25

"In all these things we are more than conquerors through him who loved us. For I am sure that neither death, nor life, nor angels, nor principalities, nor things present, nor things to come, nor powers, nor height, nor depth, nor anything else in all creation, will be able to separate us from the love of God in Christ Jesus our Lord."
—Romans 8:37–38

St. Thomas More by H. Holbein © Restored Traditions. Used with permission.

Closing Prayer

O Lord,
give us a mind that is humble, quiet, peaceable, patient, and charitable, and a taste of your Holy Spirit in all our thoughts, words, and deeds.

O Lord,
give us a lively faith, a firm hope,
a fervent charity, and a love of you.

Take from us all lukewarmness in meditation and all dullness in prayer.
Give us fervor and delight in thinking of you, your grace, and your tender compassion toward us.

Give us, good Lord,
the grace to work for the things we pray for.
Amen.

—Saint Thomas More
Saint Thomas More, pray for us.

SESSION 1 - SAINT THOMAS MORE

EXCERPT FROM THE BOOK *TRUE REFORMERS:*

"I die the King's good servant, but God's first." —Saint Thomas More

In the year 2010, on a visit to the United Kingdom, Pope Benedict XVI was invited to speak to the House of Commons. Assembled before him were the members of Parliament, all the living prime ministers, and the Anglican and Catholic bishops of England along with other invited notables. Early in his address, Benedict singled out one statesmen from England's long parliamentary history as worthy of special honor:

> As I speak to you in this historic setting, I think of the countless men and women down the centuries who have played their part in the momentous events that have taken place within these walls and have shaped the lives of many generations of Britons, and others besides. In particular, I recall the figure of Saint Thomas More, the great English scholar and statesman, who is admired by believers and non-believers alike for the integrity with which he followed his conscience, even at the cost of displeasing the sovereign whose "good servant" he was, because he chose to serve God first (Pope Benedict XVI, "Meeting with the Representatives of British Society," Westminster Hall, Sept. 17, 2010).

—Jerome K. Williams, *True Reformers* (Greenwood Village, Colorado: Augustine Institute, 2017), p. 35.

NOTES

NOTES

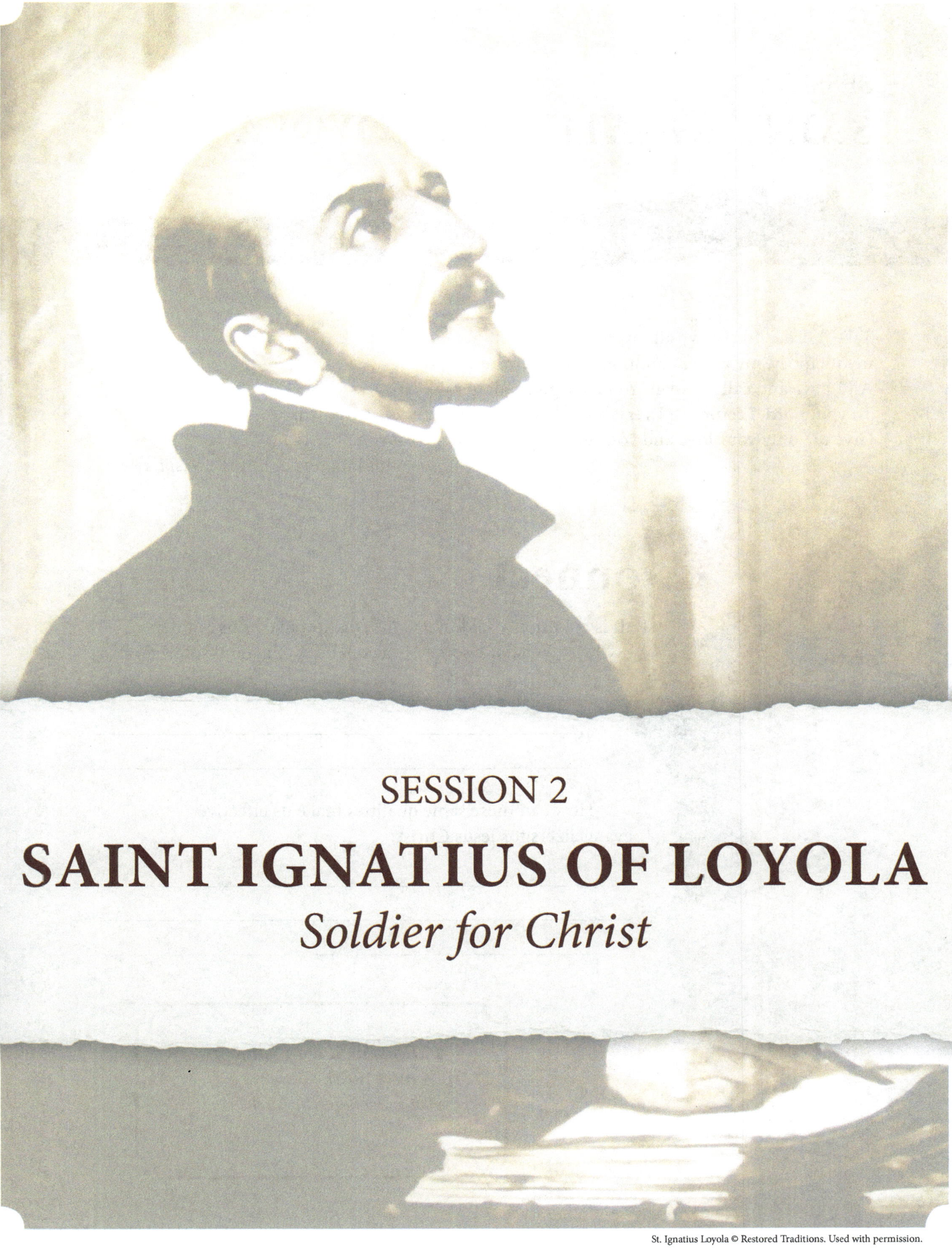

SESSION 2
SAINT IGNATIUS OF LOYOLA
Soldier for Christ

St. Ignatius Loyola © Restored Traditions. Used with permission.

SESSION 2
SAINT IGNATIUS OF LOYOLA

OPENING PRAYER

Take, Lord, and receive all my liberty,
my memory, my understanding, and my entire will,
All I have and call my own. You have given all to me.
To you, Lord, I return it. Everything is yours; do with it what you will.
Give me only your love and your grace, that is enough for me.
—Saint Ignatius of Loyola, *Suspice*

Connect

1. It is commonly said that Confirmation makes us Soldiers of Christ. What are some of the qualities of a good soldier?

   _____
   _____
   _____

2. How can these same qualities make us effective evangelizers for Jesus Christ?

   _____
   _____
   _____

> *"I have fought the good fight,
> I have finished the race,
> I have kept the faith."*
> —2 Timothy 4:7

Saint Ignatius Loyola image by Molly Sweeney. © 2017 Augustine Institute. All rights reserved

Introduction

While Martin Luther's interior troubles plunged Europe into a maelstrom of controversy, confusion, and war, the Basque soldier Ignacio de Loyola set out on an extraordinary interior pilgrimage of grace. Taught directly by God, Ignatius offered the Church a new spirituality of devoted service to Christ and founded a religious order dedicated to evangelization, the Jesuits.

Video

The following is a brief outline of the topics covered in the video teaching.

I. Conversion of St. Ignatius
   A. 30 years old when he converted
   B. From soldier of his country to soldier of Christ
   C. Injured during Battle of Pamplona
      1. During recovery read *Life of Christ* and about the lives of the saints
      2. Life transformed through reading
         a. Jesus—king, leader worth following
         b. Saints—courageous men fighting a spiritual battle
      3. Visitation from Our Lady—devoted himself to defending Mary
   D. Time in Manresa
      1. Flooded with divine illumination—taught by God
      2. Now he contemplated the things of God

II. Intellectual and Spiritual Formation
   A. Pilgrimage to Holy Land to preach—sent away by the Franciscans
   B. Told by Dominicans he needed to study theology

III. Founding of the Jesuits
   A. Beginnings
      1. Meets with young men he is studying with
      2. Takes a vow on Montmartre to be a band of companions
      3. Ordained in Venice
   B. At age 50, Ignatius founds Jesuit Order
   C. Purpose
      1. To be a new fighting force for Church
      2. Seek to preach the Gospel of Christ
   D. High ideal of service—nobility and magnanimity

IV. St. Ignatius's Writings
   A. *The Spiritual Exercises*
      1. Revealed to him at Manresa
      2. Leads souls to follow Christ
      3. Administers *Exercises* to his own men and others
      4. The Principle and Foundation—"man is created to praise, reverence, and serve God our Lord."
      5. Forms a life of integrity
   B. Meditation on the Two Standards
      1. Two armies: one lead by Lucifer, one by Christ
      2. We must decide which leader we will follow
      3. Jesuit example: follow Christ to the ends of the earth

Discuss

1. It was a cannonball that shattered the leg of Iñigo (Ignacio) Lopez de Loyola and changed the course of his life. With six months of recovery and only two books to read, *The Life of Christ* and *The Golden Legend,* a collection of the lives of the saints, something unexpected happened—Iñigo became keenly aware of the interior movements of his heart and found himself drawn to a life with God. His observations from intense prayer and his experience of consolation and desolation led him to develop the Spiritual Exercises and Rules of Discernment that are widely used among spiritual directors and the faithful today.

The *Catechism of the Catholic Church* teaches that "prayer is a vital necessity" [2744] and quotes Saint Alphonsus Liguori, who wrote: "Those who pray are certainly saved; those who do not pray are certainly damned." In your view, why is prayer necessary for salvation, and how would you describe what this kind of prayer looks like?

_____

_____

_____

2. Saint Ignatius was struck by the Person of Jesus Christ when reading about his life. He became convinced that he was the King of Kings, God in the flesh, to whom he should entrust his loyal service as a soldier. Jesus was no longer just a historical figure, but was now his Savior, his Lord, his friend. Inspired by the faith of the saints, Ignatius wrote: "Saint Francis did this, so I must do it. Saint Dominic did this, so I must do it."

The *Catechism* defines faith as "[entrusting] oneself wholly to God and [believing] absolutely what he says" [150]. In other words, faith involves a surrender of both our will and intellect. How do the saints show us what true faith is, and what prevents us from imitating them?

_____

_____

_____

3. Saint Ignatius experienced joy and enthusiasm when he meditated on *The Life of Christ* and *The Golden Legend.* This consolation clarified a sense of meaning and purpose for his life. On the other hand, when he reflected on his previous desires to be a great knight, to win the heart of a noble lady, and to serve his country, he experienced doubt and anxiety.

The Church teaches that Jesus Christ "fully reveals man to himself and makes his supreme calling clear" (*Gaudium et Spes* 22). How do you think Jesus reveals to you a deeper understanding of yourself and your purpose in life?

_____

_____

_____

SESSION 2 - SAINT IGNATIUS OF LOYOLA

4. Saint Ignatius's devotion to Mary began during his convalescence when he had a vision of Mary with the child Jesus. The image of her love, joy, and tenderness endeared his heart. He would later invite retreatants in the Spiritual Exercises to imagine themselves with Mary at the Annunciation, Nativity, at the foot of the Cross, and at the empty tomb. Saint Ignatius understood that a relationship with Mary would draw him closer to God.

How would you respond to someone who says "Catholics are guilty of idolatry in the way they regard Mary because the Bible nowhere instructs us to revere, pray to, or rely on anyone other than God"?

_____

_____

_____

5. Unlike his contemporaries, Saint Teresa of Ávila and Saint John of the Cross, who wrote beautiful spiritual treatises and mystical poetry, Saint Ignatius wrote *The Spiritual Exercises* as a book of directions for one person to guide another through a series of spiritual activities. It is essentially a manual for a 30-day silent retreat that begins with "The First Principle and Foundation," which reads:

> Man is created to praise, reverence, and serve God Our Lord, and by doing so, to save his soul. All other things on the face of the earth are created for man in order to help him pursue the end for which he is created. It follows from this that he must use other created things, in so far as they help towards one's end, and free oneself from them, in so far as they are obstacles to one's end. To do this, we need to make ourselves indifferent to all created things, provided the matter is subject to our free choice and there is no other prohibition. Thus, as far as we are concerned, we should not want health more than illness, wealth more than poverty, fame more than disgrace, a long life more than a short one, and similarly for all the rest, but we should desire and choose only what helps us more towards the end for which we are created.

St. Ignatius of Loyola by P. Rubens © Restored Traditions. Used with permission.

To begin the Spiritual Exercises, Saint Ignatius proposes a major consideration. How would you put that consideration into your own words?

_____

_____

_____

_____

6. A key meditation in *The Spiritual Exercises* is called "A Meditation on the Two Standards"—a "standard" being a flag. All of us have a decision to make. We either stand under the flag of Christ, or we stand with world, which is under the power of the devil. The *Catechism* teaches: "This dramatic situation of the whole world [which] is in the power of the evil one makes man's life a battle" [409].

The movie *Silence*, based upon the Shusaku Endo novel of the same name, takes place in seventeenth century Japan during a time of fierce persecution of the Catholic Faith. Based on true events, the story illustrates the strategy of the shogunate (military rule) to rid the influence of Christianity in Japan. Knowing that martyrdom only served to strengthen the Church, as the death of Saint Paul Miki and his twenty-five companions demonstrated, they aimed to get the Jesuit priests to apostatize and thus lead the Japanese Catholics to do the same. Under horrific torture of himself and other faithful Japanese Catholics, Fr. Cristóvão Ferreira does apostatize and assimilates into Japanese beliefs and customs. Under his influence, Fr. Rodrigues does the same.

Miracles of St. Ignatius Loyola by P. Rubens © Restored Traditions. Used with permission.

The movie/book poses a thought-provoking question: Would Jesus, in view of his mercy, want us to publicly renounce our faith in him that we might save ourselves, as well as others, from torture and death? How would you answer that question taking into consideration Saint Ignatius's "two standards"?

_____
_____
_____
_____
_____
_____

"You must make a sacrifice of yourself continuously, for the glory of God and the salvation and well-being of others, not just a matter of general orientation, but throwing your whole life and everything you do into this enterprise."
—Saint Ignatius of Loyola

Commit

The genius of Saint Ignatius's method of prayer is its emphasis on growing in self-awareness. For example, paying greater attention to the affective movements of our hearts and bringing those to Jesus in our prayer facilitates greater intimacy with God, healing, and discernment. The commitment this week is to have a Holy Hour before Jesus, invite the Holy Spirit to help you become more aware of your heart, and write those thoughts, feelings, and desires down in a journal. Commit to have an ongoing conversation with Jesus about these very things.

"For though we live in the world we are not carrying on a worldly war, for the weapons of our warfare are not worldly but have divine power to destroy strongholds."
—2 Corinthians 10:3–4

St. Ignatius of Loyola by Domenichino © Restored Traditions. Used with permission.

Closing Prayer

The Anima Christi

Soul of Christ, sanctify me.
Body of Christ, save me.
Blood of Christ, inebriate me.
Water from Christ's side, wash me.
Passion of Christ, strengthen me.
O good Jesus, hear me.
Within Thy wounds hide me.
Suffer me not to be separated from Thee.
From the malicious enemy defend me.
In the hour of my death call me
And bid me come unto Thee
That I may praise Thee with Thy saints
and with Thy angels
Forever and ever.
Amen.

—Saint Ignatius of Loyola
Saint Ignatius of Loyola, pray for us.

EXCERPT FROM THE BOOK *TRUE REFORMERS*:

"Go and set the world on fire!" —Saint Ignatius of Loyola

The year 1521 was notable for more than Ignatius's conversion. It was the year that Hernan Cortes, a man of roughly the same age and social background as Ignatius, completed the conquest of Tenochtitlan and the Aztec empire, opening a new chapter in Spanish and European history. It was also the year in which Martin Luther, having written three widely-read tracts against the Catholic Church, refused to retract his positions before the imperial general assembly, or Diet, at Worms, thereby effectively initiating the Protestant Reformation. These momentous events did much to shape the world into which Ignatius would throw his considerable energies as a missionary and reformer of the Church. He later said, "I do not consider myself as having retired from military service, but only as having come under the orders of God."

—Jerome K. Williams, *True Reformers* (Greenwood Village, Colorado: Augustine Institute, 2017), pp. 62–63.

NOTES

SESSION 3

SAINT PHILIP NERI
The Apostle of Joy

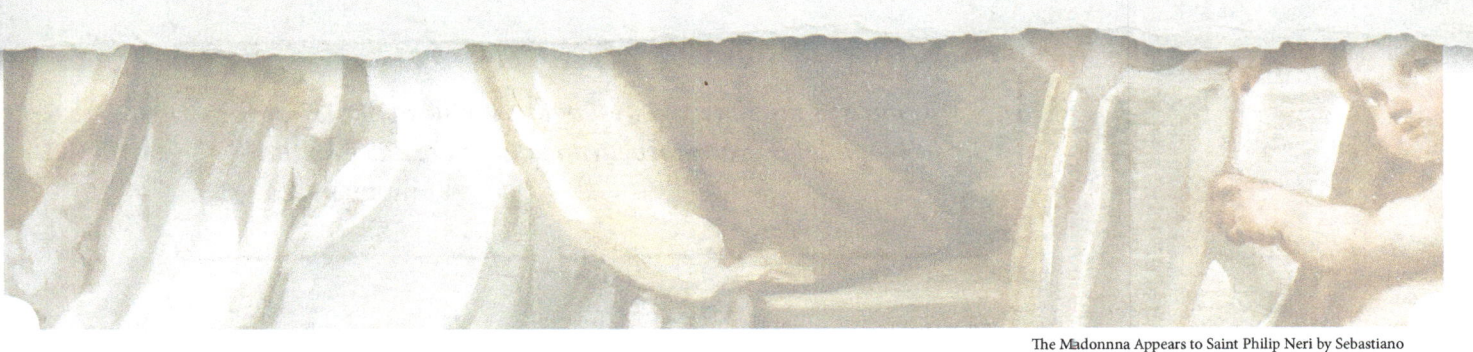

The Madonnna Appears to Saint Philip Neri by Sebastiano
© Restored Traditions. Used with permission.

SESSION 3
SAINT PHILIP NERI

OPENING PRAYER

My Lord Jesus, I want to love You but You cannot trust me.
If You do not help me, I will never do any good.
I do not know You; I look for You but I do not find You.
Come to me, O Lord.
If I knew You, I would also know myself.
If I have never loved You before, I want to love You truly now.
I want to do Your will alone; putting no trust in myself,
I hope in You, O Lord.
Amen.

—Saint Philip Neri

Connect

1. Many of the saints were known for their great sense of humor and for not taking themselves too seriously. What are the benefits of being a light-hearted person?

   _____
   _____

2. How can true humility help us to bring others to Christ?

   _____
   _____

> "Rejoice in the Lord always; again I will say, Rejoice. Let all men know your forbearance. The Lord is at hand."
> —Philippians 4:4–5

SESSION 3 - SAINT PHILIP NERI

Introduction

To a Rome ravaged by war and wearied by the decadence of the Renaissance popes, Saint Philip Neri came as an unlikely reformer. Mystic, hermit, prankster, and effortless leader of men, Neri had a great sense of humor and an even greater heart. His creative response to the challenge of the Reformation era made him the Apostle of Rome.

Video

The following is a brief outline of the topics covered in the video teaching.

I. **St. Philip Neri's Early Years**
   A. Florentine by birth
   B. Inspired by the Dominican preacher Savonarola
   C. Obedient and cheerful child
   D. In order to follow call of Christ, headed to Rome

II. **Life in Rome**
   A. Filled with wealthy cardinals, disappointing popes, and immoral people
   B. Lived as a hermit in the city
   C. Visit from God as a ball of fire
      1. Resulted in the enlargement of heart
      2. "I am wounded by love" (Song of Songs 2:5)
   D. Gathered young men to teach the Gospel: "My friends, when shall we begin to do good?"

III. **St. Philip as a Priest**
   A. Great confessor
   B. New kind of priesthood: interior, thoughtful men
   C. 1575: Congregation of the Oratory
      1. One rule: charity
      2. "If you want to rule well, have few rules"
      3. Renewal of the priesthood
   D. Desire to be a missionary
      1. Seeks counsel of Carthusian
      2. Response: "Rome will be your India"

IV. **Pilgrims in Rome**
   A. Neri served the pilgrims
   B. Led them in prayer, spiritual talks, singing hymns, and fasting
   C. Seven Churches Pilgrimage

V. **The Apostle of Joy**
   A. Holy virtue through holy cheerfulness
   B. Mortify your reason—don't take yourself too seriously
   C. Philip acted the fool: did not want to be revered and imitated
   D. Pranks as penance

Discuss

1. Philip Neri came to Rome as a young layman. He spent his nights praying deep down in the catacombs of Saint Sebastian. It was on one of these nights that Philip had an extraordinary experience with the Holy Spirit. A ball of fire appeared to him, entered his mouth, moved down into his chest, and created such a burning sensation that he threw himself onto the cool floor to ease the heat. This event physically changed his heart. After his ordination to the priesthood, penitents could hear his heart beating in the confessional and feel heat emanating from his body. Upon his death, the autopsy revealed an abnormally enlarged heart with two ribs moved out of place to accommodate it.

What are we to make of this extraordinary experience, and does it offer any illumination on the purpose and destiny of our bodies?

_____
_____
_____

2. Saint Philip Neri's heart was full of the love of God after his powerful experience with the Holy Spirit. He would go to the hospitals to visit the sick, taught religion to children, and would talk to anyone on the streets about Jesus, from beggars to bankers. He also worked tirelessly to spread the Forty Hours Devotion. The devotion, which is employed especially during times of war or disease, solemnly exposes the Blessed Sacrament for forty hours for adoration by the faithful. His passionate preaching during the Forty Hours Devotions brought about many conversions. Historians have suggested that the lack of penetration of Protestantism into Rome was largely due to the influence of Saint Philip Neri.

Saint Philip Neri wrote, "Our sweet Jesus, through the excess of his love and liberality, has left himself to us in the Most Holy Sacrament." And yet, approximately half of American Catholics are unaware of the Church's teaching on the Real Presence of Jesus in the Eucharist as the "source and summit of the Christian life" [CCC 1324]. In your opinion, why is this the case, and what could be done to remedy the situation?

_____
_____
_____
_____
_____

St. Philip Neri portrait by Guido Reni (ca. 1614) Saint's Chapel, Chiesa Nuova, Rome, Italy © futureGalore, Shutterstock.com

3. In the year 1520, Martin Luther wrote to Pope Leo X: "I have rightly cursed your see, called the Roman Curia, which neither you nor any human being can deny is more corrupt than Babylon or Sodom and, as far as I can tell, is composed of depraved, desperate, and notorious godlessness" (*On the Freedom of the Christian*, 22–24). Thirteen years later Saint Philip Neri arrived in Rome. Contrary to Luther, he refused to call attention to the corruption in the hierarchy. Rather, he worked to win back worldly clergy and influence seminarians by living out his priesthood with joy and simplicity. Frequent confession, daily mental prayer, and spiritual direction were his prescription.

How would you counsel a family member or friend who was determined to leave the Catholic Church because of moral failures within the leadership?

_____
_____
_____

4. Saint Philip Neri understood that humility is the gateway to abundant life in Christ. He wrote: "The skin of self-love is fastened strongly on our hearts, and it hurts to flay it off. And the more we get down to the quick of it, to what is real in our hearts, the sharper and more difficult it is to bear." In other words, our insecurities and fear of humiliation comes from a false self, not our true selves. This is the reason he would wear ridiculous clothes, shave off half his beard, and carry weeds and smell them. When a man asked Philip if he could wear a hair shirt, Philip gave him permission with one condition—he had to wear the hair shirt outside his clothes. He was intent on helping people not take themselves too seriously and he would teach that sincere and frequent Confession was needed to obtain humility.

Humility is not thinking less of yourself, but thinking of yourself less! What does this mean to you and why is humility needed to acquire true peace and joy?

_____
_____
_____

5. Saint Philip Neri led a prayer group for young people known as the Oratory. They would gather in his home each week to read and discuss Sacred Scripture, pray, sing hymns, and hear a short teaching called a *ferverino*. Above all, he taught them how to pray with the Scriptures and interpret them within the Sacred Tradition of the Church. On the contrary, Martin Luther and his movement were championing *sola Scriptura*, which is Latin for "Bible alone." This was a totally new approach to how Sacred Scripture was read. They no longer looked to the Church as the guide to interpreting Scripture, but only the individual's conscience.

Why should we look to the Church for the correct interpretation of Scripture, and how would you articulate this to a "Bible only" Christian?

_____
_____
_____

6. There is a pattern of practice among saintly priests—they spent hours upon hours every day hearing confessions. Similarly, there is a pattern of practice among saintly men and women—they went to Confession frequently, often once a week. It should come as no surprise that Saint Philip Neri, who so much loved the Real Presence of Jesus in the Holy Eucharist, would be so devoted to helping men and women through the Sacrament of Reconciliation to receive Jesus worthily and love him as he deserves to be loved.

The Madonna Appears to St. Philip Neri by Sebastiano
© Restored Traditions. Used with permission.

You might think that the saints would have needed the Sacrament of Reconciliation less as they grew in sanctity. And yet, the opposite was the case. Why do you think that is?

_____
_____
_____
_____
_____
_____

"I think it is very important to be able to see the humorous side of life and its joyful dimension and not to take everything too tragically. I would also say it is necessary for my ministry. A writer once said that angels can fly because they do not take themselves too seriously. Maybe we could also fly a bit if we didn't think we were so important."
—Pope Benedict XVI

Commit

Saint Philip Neri believed strongly in frequent Confession and so he made himself readily available to penitents in the confessional. The commitment this week is to make ourselves accountable to someone who will make sure we are going to the Sacrament of Reconciliation regularly, at least once a month. Who will be that person for you?

"We are not saints yet, but we, too, should beware. Uprightness and virtue do have their rewards, in self-respect and in respect from others, and it is easy to find ourselves aiming for the result rather than the cause. Let us aim for joy, rather than respectability. Let us make fools of ourselves from time to time, and thus see ourselves, for a moment, as the all-wise God sees us."

—Saint Philip Neri

Closing Prayer

Rejoicing always in all things,
gain for me the grace of
perfect resignation to [Your] will,
of indifference to matters of this world,
and a constant sight of Heaven,
so that I may never be disappointed
at the Divine providences,
never desponding, never sad, never fretful,
that my countenance may always
be open and cheerful,
and my words kind and pleasant,
as becomes those who,
in whatever state of life they are,
have the greatest of all goods,
the favor of [You],
and the prospect of eternal bliss.

—Blessed John Henry Cardinal Newman
Saint Philip Neri, pray for us.

St. Philip Neri Italian Baroque Sculpture in Mafra National Palace and Covent in Portugal © StockPhotosArt, Shutterstock.com

EXCERPT FROM THE BOOK *TRUE REFORMERS*:

"Well, friends. When shall we have a mind to begin to do good?" —Saint Phillip Neri

[The] saintly quality of resolving opposites into an integrated personality is emphatically present in Philip Neri: the desert father in the midst of bustling Rome, the practical joker whom everyone took seriously, the admirer of the grim reformer Savonarola who wooed souls with sweetness, the lover of obedience who cherished personal freedom, the austere ascetic who loved to see people around him enjoying life, the profound mystic who put little stock in spiritual experience, the man who saw the best in everyone else and detected a devil in himself. Yet there is hardly a historical character who is more recognizably whole, more completely himself, than Neri. He wrote little, and he established a religious congregation almost by accident. But the city where he spent most of his life has not been able to forget the imprint of his personality. He belongs to the Eternal City as truly as its piazzas and its dishes of pasta. Rome would not be quite itself without Philip leading his hundreds to the Seven Churches, laughing and praying with his companions among the streets and hills, and haunting the steps of the great basilicas in the quiet of the night as he read his solitary prayers by moonlight.

—Jerome K. Williams, *True Reformers* (Greenwood Village, Colorado: Augustine Institute, 2017), pp. 103–104.

NOTES

_____
_____
_____
_____
_____
_____
_____
_____
_____

SESSION 4
SAINT CHARLES BORROMEO
The Good Shepherd

St. Charles Borromeo Meditating on the Crucifix by Tiepolo
© Restored Traditions. Used with permission.

SESSION 4
SAINT CHARLES BORROMEO

OPENING PRAYER

Almighty Father, you have generously made known to us
the mysteries of your life through Jesus Christ your Son in the Holy Spirit.
Enlighten my mind to know these mysteries
which your Church treasures and teaches.
Move my heart to love them and my will to live in accord with them.
Let me realize that I am simply your instrument for bringing others to this knowledge.
Help me to be faithful to this task that you have entrusted to me.
Through Christ our Lord.
Amen.

Connect

1. The Church calls us to a life of simplicity and penance. What are some benefits of detaching ourselves from material things?

   _____
   _____

2. What are some practical ways you could try to live more simply? How might this impact your spiritual life?

   _____
   _____

> "Love, and practice simplicity and humility, and don't worry about the opinion of the world because if the world had nothing to say against us, we would not be real servants of God."
> —Saint Padre Pio

Saint Charles Borromeo image by Molly Sweeney. ©
2017 Augustine Institute. All rights reserved

SESSION 4 - SAINT CHARLES BORROMEO

Introduction

As the Cardinal-nephew of Pope Pius IV, Saint Charles Borromeo was one of the wealthiest and most powerful men in all of Rome. Yet he chose the extraordinary challenge of reforming the enormous Archdiocese of Milan to the pampered life of a Renaissance prince, and willingly spent himself in the service of his flock.

Video

The following is a brief outline of the topics covered in the video teaching.

I. St. Charles's Early Years
   A. Second son of a nobleman destined for priesthood
   B. Age 12 became abbot of a monastery
   C. Nephew of pope, Charles elevated to cardinalate at young age

II. Borromeo in Rome
   A. Clergy lived luxurious lives
      1. Borromeo given several titles and roles
      2. Uncomfortable with lavish lifestyle
      3. Lived a state of detachment
   B. Influenced by St. Philip Neri and the Jesuits
   C. Involvement in Council of Trent
      1. Not present, but impacted the proceedings
      2. Cardinal Seripando
   D. Set to reform bishops and clergy
      1. Seminary—place for diocese to educate
      2. St. Charles established first seminary

III. New Priesthood
   A. Discipline and spiritual depth
   B. St. Charles pressured not to pursue priesthood after death of his brother
   C. Borromeo committed to priesthood

IV. Life as Archbishop
   A. Becomes Archbishop of Milan
   B. Milan—incredibly large diocese
   C. Borromeo continued a simple life while surrounded by luxury
      1. Enforced monastic rules in his household
      2. Challenged wealthy priests to do likewise
   D. Path of reform: cathedral → parishes in Milan → parishes outlying diocese
   E. Liberty of Gospel: enable a pastor to enter into the life of his people

V. The Heroism of St. Charles Borromeo
   A. 1576: Bubonic Plague hit Milan
   B. Borromeo emphasized the healing presence of Christ
      1. Set up 19 altars throughout the city for the sick
      2. Frequently visited the sick and dying
   C. Shared his life of prayer, poverty of spirit, generosity, and hard work

Discuss

1. In Matthew 23:1–3, Jesus says to the crowds and to his disciples, "The scribes and the Pharisees sit on Moses' seat; so practice and observe whatever they tell you, but not what they do; for they preach, but do not practice." This is a difficult teaching because Jesus is asking for obedience to an office of authority, in this case Moses's seat, even when the person in that office is guilty of hypocrisy. Similarly, Jesus established an authoritative Church when he gave the "keys of the Kingdom of Heaven" to Peter even though he knew that those invested with authority were not always going to live up to the responsibilities of their office.

The true reformers were obedient to the Church at a time when the authority of the Church was greatly challenged. Why is obedience a necessary virtue for Christian discipleship?

_____
_____
_____

2. In Matthew 19:16–22, the rich young man approached Jesus and asked what he must do to have eternal life. Jesus asked him to sell all his possessions, give his proceeds to the poor, and follow him. The young man walked away sad because Jesus had asked for more than he was willing to give. Saint Charles Borromeo, on the other hand, descended from a noble and wealthy family of Lombardy and yet was detached from his wealth. He was known for his simple and austere life at a time of excess among some of the leadership in the Church. When he became the Archbishop of Milan, one of his first actions was to give much of his personal property to the poor.

What did Saint Charles Borromeo understand that the rich young man in Matthew's Gospel did not?

_____
_____
_____

3. Saint Charles would meditate upon the crucifix in his prayer. He called the crucifix a *cathedra*, which is Latin for chair. *Cathedra* is the symbol of the bishop's teaching authority in the Church. In other words, Saint Charles was saying that Jesus was no greater a teacher than when he was hanging on the Cross.

What does the crucifix tell us about the meaning and purpose of our lives?

_____
_____
_____

SESSION 4 - SAINT CHARLES BORROMEO

4. The Council of Trent defended and reaffirmed many of the teachings that were under attack by the Protestants: indulgences; the seven deuterocanonical books of the Bible; the Seven Sacraments; justification by faith and works; Sacred Tradition and Sacred Scripture as the Deposit of Faith; communion under one species; transubstantiation; Original Sin; Purgatory; and Masses for the dead. On the reform side, Trent reaffirmed priestly celibacy, prioritized good preaching, called for bishops and pastors to reside within their areas of responsibility, and established seminaries for the thorough formation of clergy.

In 1559 Angelo Medici, the uncle of Saint Charles Borromeo, was elected pope and took the name of Pius IV. He made Charles Borromeo a cardinal and secretary of state between 1560 and 1567. Ordained to the priesthood in 1563, the pope asked Charles to preside at the Council of Trent and to oversee its implementation. In your estimation, why was Cardinal Borromeo the right man for these times?

_____
_____
_____

5. Evangelization and catechesis are relational because people don't care how much you know until they know how much you care. In other words, an effective evangelist and catechist meets people where they are and earns the right to be heard.

How did Saint Charles Borromeo, as the archbishop of the largest diocese in the world at that time, embody these principles of evangelization and catechesis?

_____
_____
_____

6. Saint Charles Borromeo could have led a life of ease. He was born into privilege and wealth. He could have used his family connections to his advantage and never worked or seriously engaged in the challenges of his time. But Charles understood he was not made for comfort, he was made for greatness. He overcame a speech impediment as a child, worked hard to get through school with little to no financial assistance, willingly embraced major responsibilities as a young man, exhibited servant leadership in his powerful positions, gave generously to the poor, risked his health serving those afflicted with the plague, and worked tirelessly to strengthen the Church.

In a nationwide study of college students done at the University of Texas, over one-half admitted to having thoughts of taking their own lives. Charles Borromeo understood from a very young age that his life was not his own. How can we help young people today understand that their lives are not their own?

_____
_____
_____

Commit

Saint Charles Borromeo was very generous with his personal property. The commitment this week is to evaluate how we are doing with our personal stewardship. The goal is to commit to regular tithing and service. What is one change you can make to be more generous?

"Draw near to God and he will draw near to you. Cleanse your hands, you sinners, and purify your hearts, you men of double mind . . . Humble yourselves before the Lord and he will exalt you."
—James 4:8–10

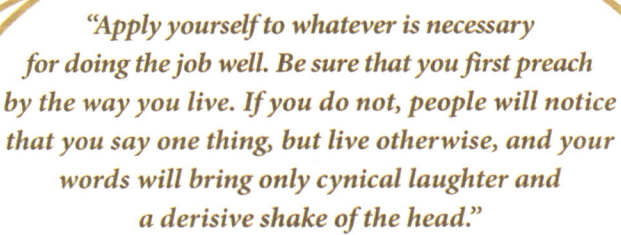

"Apply yourself to whatever is necessary for doing the job well. Be sure that you first preach by the way you live. If you do not, people will notice that you say one thing, but live otherwise, and your words will bring only cynical laughter and a derisive shake of the head."
—Saint Charles Borromeo

Closing Prayer

Almighty Father, inspired by the example
of Saint Charles Borromeo
and guided by the Holy Spirit, may we become imitators of Christ and faithful
followers of him Crucified.
Replenish us with the spirit of the Apostles,
who were consumed with zeal for your glory,
untiring in their labors
for the light and support of the Church in the world,
and most desirous of the salvation of souls
as models of humility and penance.
Amen.

Saint Charles Borromeo, pray for us.

St. Charles Borromeo Giving Alms to the Poor by Giordano
© Restored Traditions. Used with permission.

SESSION 4 - SAINT CHARLES BORROMEO

EXCERPT FROM THE BOOK *TRUE REFORMERS*:

"I am now wedded to the spouse I have so long desired." —Saint Charles Borromeo

Because the Church is a sacramental body, any genuine reform of the Church will touch all aspects of her being, both human and divine. While true reform begins with the invisible renewal of the individual heart and mind, it does not end there; it gathers up and transforms the visible workings of Christ's Body as well: her rites, her government, her customs, her music and architecture, all the complex weave of institutional life that allows Christ to be concretely present in the world. This does not mean that reform is necessarily, or even usually, a "top-down" affair. The Holy Spirit seems to take delight in using unlikely instruments for accomplishing his designs. But if reform often begins with the lowly and the obscure and is supported by the hidden mystical union of the soul with God, it always, by necessity, finds its way into the existential aspects of the Church's communal life.

Practically speaking, given God's chosen form for his Body, this means that reform needs to reach the apostolic leaders of the Church: priests, and especially bishops and popes.

—Jerome K. Williams, *True Reformers* (Greenwood Village, Colorado: Augustine Institute, 2017), p. 125.

NOTES

NOTES

SESSION 5

SAINT TERESA OF ÁVILA
A Study in Perseverence

St. Teresa of Ávila by G. Honthorst © Restored Traditions. Used with permission.

SESSION 5
SAINT TERESA OF ÁVILA

OPENING PRAYER

O my God! Source of all mercy! I acknowledge Your sovereign power.
While recalling the wasted years that are past,
I believe that You, Lord, can in an instant turn this loss to gain.
Miserable as I am, yet I firmly believe that You can do all things.
Please restore to me the time lost, giving me Your grace,
both now and in the future,
that I may appear before You in "wedding garments."
Amen

St. Teresa, pray for us.

—Saint Teresa

onnect

1. What are some of your greatest strengths? How could you use these strengths for the Kingdom of God?

   _____
   _____

2. What effect might you have on family, friends, or colleagues if you strived to live a life more pleasing to God?

   _____
   _____

> "For God alone my soul waits in silence,
> for my hope is from him. He only is my rock and my
> salvation, my fortress; I shall not be shaken.
> On God rests my deliverance and my honor;
> my mighty rock, my refuge is God."
> —Psalm 62:5–7

Saint Teresa of Ávila image by Molly Sweeney. © 2017 Augustine Institute. All rights reserved

Introduction

Nobly-born, wealthy, captivating, and headstrong, Teresa de Ahumada was unlikely timber for a great work of renovation. After many years of complacent living in a fashionable convent, Teresa was drawn into a mystical embrace and learned directly from Divine Inspiration what a life more pleasing to God would be. She spent the last twenty years of her life in a whirlwind of activity as the founder of the Discalced or reformed branch of the Carmelites in Spain.

Video

The following is a brief outline of the topics covered in the video teaching.

I. Early Life
A. Noble family; life of comfort and ease
B. Intelligent, beautiful, captivating
C. Father opposed to religious life
   1. Teresa flees home to Carmelite convent
   2. 1535: becomes a nun at Convent of Incarnation

II. Convent of Incarnation
A. 300 nuns
B. Nuns not always there for the right reasons
C. Lax lifestyle leads to temptation. Teresa ceases to pray
D. Statue of Christ tormented
   1. Moved Teresa
   2. Moved from fear to love
   3. Develops a spirituality; devoted to prayer

III. Spiritual Transformation
A. Divine visions
B. Guidance from Saint Peter of Alcántara
C. Received a calling to reform Carmelites
   1. If God is calling you to this, he will make it happen
   2. *Solo Dios basta*—God alone suffices

IV. Reformation I: Founding of New Convent
A. Devotion to Saint Joseph
   1. Helps in all of our needs
   2. "God does whatever he commands"
B. Convent approved by authorities
C. Live according to original 12th century rule
   1. Days dedicated to prayer
   2. Receive everything from God
D. Key to religious life: humility

V. Reformation II: Carmelite Order
A. Superior from Rome sought out Teresa
B. Teresa to reform all of the Carmelites
   1. 17 reformed convents (of women)
   2. 11 reformed convents (of men)
   3. 500 men and women in Spain living under discalced rule

V. Back at Incarnation
A. Teresa established as prioress
B. Nuns not pleased with placement
   1. Demanded that they elect their own head
   2. Barred the doors when Teresa tried to come
C. Teresa places Our Lady as actual head of the convent
D. Slowly wins over the nuns
   1. Within a year—the whole convent transformed
   2. End of three years—nuns want her back as prioress
E. Teresa's lesson: true life we lead— hidden life we live with God

Discuss

1. Spain has a long tradition of being a very Catholic country. This is due in large part to eight long centuries, from the eighth to the sixteenth, when Spain had to defend itself against Muslim conquest. However, when Teresa de Cepeda y Ahumada was born on March 28, 1515, a more cultural and less vibrant Catholicism had settled in, as it had in much of Europe. The danger with cultural Catholicism is the lowering of defenses while a hidden, raging spiritual battle remains.

Saint Teresa of Ávila wrote in *Interior Castle*: "It is foolish to think that we will enter Heaven without entering into ourselves." What do you think that Saint Teresa meant by this profound statement and how does it relate to the danger of cultural Catholicism?

_____
_____
_____
_____

2. As a child Teresa had a keen interest in the lives of the saints and a zeal to become one herself. As a young woman, she entered the Carmelite Monastery of the Incarnation in Ávila with the same zeal for holiness. Sadly, she came to discover very few of her sisters shared her purity of intention.

St. Teresa of Ávila by G. Honthorst © Restored Traditions. Used with permission.

There is a story of a pastor who visited a parishioner who had stopped coming to the parish. He was invited in, but they sat without speaking in front of the fire. The pastor reached in with the tongs, picked up a brightly burning ember, and placed it alone to one side of the hearth. When it had lost its flame and heat, the pastor got up and left. He was assured that the parishioner understood his object lesson when he saw him in the pew the following Sunday.

How does this parable of the lonely ember relate to the decisions Sister Teresa made to reform religious life?

_____
_____
_____
_____
_____

3. Mysticism is a supernatural experience of union with God. At times, these mystical episodes can include phenomena such as levitation, visions, audible sensations, ecstasy, and even the stigmata. Sister Teresa was a mystic. It is no wonder that she devoted herself more and more to quiet prayer when she was having experiences of being overwhelmed by the love of God.

Pope Saint John Paul II, in his Apostolic Letter *At the Beginning of the Third Millennium*, writes of a "renewed need for prayer" [33] and points us to the "great mystical tradition of the Church" as evidence of how prayer can progress. In your opinion, how is a lay person to interpret his exhortation?

_____
_____
_____
_____

St. Teresa of Ávila Before Christ by P. Rubens © Restored Traditions. Used with permission.

4. There was an occasion where Sister Teresa was troubled with fear and anxiety. She retreated to a hermitage where she discovered an image of Jesus bound to a pillar. While meditating upon this image, she heard a gentle whisper from Jesus. Though she could not make out what he said, the fear left her, and she was at peace. She would later write this prayer:

> Let nothing disturb you,
> Let nothing frighten you,
> All things are passing away:
> God never changes.
> Patience obtains all things.
> Whoever has God lacks nothing;
> God alone suffices.

First John 4:18 reads: "There is no fear in love, but perfect love casts out fear." What do you think is the practical application of this verse to our lives?

_____
_____
_____
_____
_____
_____

5. Sister Teresa developed a strong devotion to Saint Joseph at a time in the Church when the veneration of Saint Joseph had not yet developed. She even named her new convent after him, the convent that would become the model for reform of monastic life in the Church. She had this to say about Saint Joseph in Chapter 6 of her autobiography:

> I do not remember even now that I have ever asked anything of him which he has failed to grant. I am astonished at the great favors which God has bestowed on me through this blessed saint, and at the perils from which He has freed me, both in body and in soul.

If someone were to say to you: "Why pray for the intercession of Saint Joseph when you can pray directly to Jesus? Why complicate the matter with a middle man?" How would you respond?

_____
_____
_____

6. The Provincial of the Carmelites asked Sister Teresa to become the Superior at the Carmelite Monastery of the Incarnation. Though on the brink of collapse, the embittered sisters were none too happy to have Sister Teresa return. Calling a chapter meeting the next morning, Sister Teresa placed a statue of the Blessed Virgin Mary in her seat of authority. With the assistance of John of the Cross, Sister Teresa won her sisters back to true devotion to Jesus and their vocation in just three years.

What principles of effective leadership can be drawn out from this story of Saint Teresa?

_____
_____
_____
_____
_____

> *"The soul's true greatness is in loving God and in humbling oneself in His presence, completely forgetting oneself and believing oneself to be nothing; because the Lord is great, but He is well-pleased only with the humble; He always opposes the proud."*
> —Saint Faustina, *Divine Mercy in My Soul*

Commit

Fear is not from God. It holds us back from experiencing the life Jesus has for us, life to the full. The commitment this week is to reflect honestly on our fears and to relate them to Jesus in prayer. Jesus says to us: "Let not your hearts be troubled, neither let them be afraid" (John 14:27). Consider praying daily this prayer of Saint Teresa: *Let nothing disturb you, let nothing frighten you, all things are passing away: God never changes. Patience obtains all things, whoever has God lacks nothing; God alone suffices."*

"Contemplation is a gaze of faith, fixed on Jesus. 'I look at him and he looks at me' . . . This focus on Jesus is a renunciation of self. His gaze purifies our heart; the light of the countenance of Jesus illumines the eyes of our heart and teaches us to see everything in the light of his truth and his compassion for all men. Contemplation also turns its gaze on the mysteries of the life of Christ. Thus it learns the 'interior knowledge of our Lord,' the more to love him and follow him (cf. Saint Ignatius of Loyola, Spiritual Exercises, 104)."

—CCC 2715

Closing Prayer

May today there be peace within.
May you trust God that you are exactly where you are meant to be.
May you not forget the infinite possibilities that are born of faith.
May you use those gifts that you have received,
and pass on the love that has been given to you.
May you be content knowing you are a child of God.
Let this presence settle into your bones,
and allow your soul the freedom to sing, dance, praise and love.
It is there for each and every one of us.

Let nothing disturb you,
Let nothing frighten you,
All things are passing away:
God never changes.
Patience obtains all things.
Whoever has God lacks nothing;
God alone suffices.
Amen.

Saint Teresa of Ávila, pray for us.

—Saint Teresa

St. Teresa of Ávila © Restored Traditions.
Used with permission.

EXCERPT FROM THE BOOK *TRUE REFORMERS*:

"Solo Dios basta." —Saint Teresa of Ávila

An old saying has it that the contemplative leaves the world, and then the world seeks out the contemplative. Again and again the pattern has repeated itself: an individual or a group of men or women have left normal society and have pursued solitude and poverty to follow the contemplative vocation. Like Anthony, they have penetrated the inhospitable desert or, like Benedict, have sought out lonely mountain caves. They have gone deep into the dark and untamed forests like Bruno and Bernard or, more strangely, have settled themselves on platforms high in the midst of the city like Simeon Stylites.

But wherever they have gone, however much they have attempted to flee the world, the world has followed them. Much to their surprise, contemplatives have regularly found themselves important members of their societies, surrounded by the trappings of usefulness and even of power and wealth. St. Benedict has been called the father of European civilization and not without good reason; but founding or saving a civilization was nowhere on the list of his intended achievements. It all seems to happen innocently enough, even by a kind of accident: the innate strength of a life focused on the worship of God and the mastery of the self spills over into all manner of social benefits.

—Jerome K. Williams, *True Reformers* (Greenwood Village, Colorado: Augustine Institute, 2017), pp. 103–104.

NOTES

SESSION 6

SAINT FRANCIS DE SALES
Pastor of Souls

St. Francis de Sales by Tiepolo © Restored Traditions. Used with permission.

SESSION 6
SAINT FRANCIS DE SALES

OPENING PRAYER

Lord, I am Yours, and I must belong to no one but You.
My soul is Yours, and must live only by You.
My will is Yours, and must love only for You.
I must love You as my first cause, since I am from You.
I must love You as my end and rest, since I am for You.
I must love You more than my own being, since my being subsists by You.
I must love You more than myself, since I am all Yours and all in You.
Amen.

—Saint Francis de Sales

Connect

1. Working on developing our human virtues is a lifetime task. What virtues can help you further your relationship with others?

   _____
   _____

2. What can you do to strengthen these virtues?

   _____
   _____

> "Let love be genuine; hate what is evil, hold fast to what is good; love one another with brotherly affection; outdo one another in showing honor. Never flag in zeal, be aglow with the Spirit, serve the Lord. Rejoice in your hope, be patient in tribulation, be constant in prayer. Contribute to the needs of the saints, practice hospitality."
> —Romans 12:9–13

Introduction

Determined from his youth to pursue the priesthood, Saint Francis de Sales lived a storied life as a priest and missionary before settling down to the duties of a small-town bishop in the foothills of the French Alps. The spiritual writings of this beloved teacher of everyday holiness are justly celebrated. In his doctrine, we find the summation of the teaching of the Catholic Reformation.

Video

The following is a brief outline of the topics covered in the video teaching.

I. St. Francis's Upbringing
   A. Prepared for a career as judge/senator
   B. Tutor introduced him to study of theology
   C. Problem of Predestination
      1. Causes Francis to despair
      2. Conversion from praying *Memorare*
      3. Loving confidence in the Father
   D. Determined to be a priest—but father opposed
   E. Help of Bishop of Geneva
      1. Wants Francis to be lead priest in diocese
      2. Father agrees to Francis's ordination

II. Life as a Priest
   A. "We must take back Geneva"
   B. Francis's plan: go on the offensive
      1. Goes to Chablais on a missionary effort
         a. Shifting of religious regime
         b. Catholics not practicing the Faith
         c. Four years of Francis
         d. Entire region came back to Catholicism
         e. Conversion through charity—not force
   C. Francis gains the admiration of King Henry IV
      1. Wants Francis to be bishop in Paris
      2. Response: no—Francis devoted to current diocese
   D. Friendship with St. Jane Frances de Chantal
   E. Inspired by Saint Charles Borromeo

III. Francis as Spiritual Director
   A. Wanted to share understanding of spiritual life
   B. Manual of spiritual life
      1. Written for one of his directees
      2. "This must be published for the good of souls"
      3. Becomes *Introduction to the Devout Life*
   C. Emphasis on meekness, patience, and humility
   D. Marks of de Sales's spirituality
      1. Patience—heart of spirituality
      2. Practicality
      3. Use of imagery

iscuss

1. Iconoclasm, which means "image breaking," became rooted in Protestantism largely due to John Calvin. Calvin wrote in his *Institutes of the Christian Religion*: "We must cling to this principle: God's glory is corrupted by an impious falsehood whenever any form is attached to him" [1.11.1]. And, in his mind, these images violated God's commandment: "You shall not make for yourself a graven image" (Exodus 20:4). Calvin felt so strongly that he devoted three chapters to this issue in his *Institutes*.

John Calvin argued that we cannot come to know God through created things but only through Scripture. What is the Catholic position on this matter?

_____
_____
_____

2. The Reformation was an age of great confusion. It can be difficult to understand why holy things were destroyed out of righteous anger. The Eleanor Cross, for example, at the intersection in Cheapside, London, was repeatedly vandalized, stripped of Catholic images, and eventually demolished. It had become a symbol of the Catholic Church, which the reformers had identified as the antichrist of biblical prophecy. Even today, many fundamentalist Christians identify the Catholic Church as the antichrist.

Jesus's high priestly prayer in John chapter 17 is for unity among his followers: "Holy Father, keep them in thy name, which thou hast given me, that they may be one, even as we are one" (v.11). In what ways is Saint Francis de Sales a model for us as someone who worked for and achieved unity in a time of painful division?

_____
_____
_____

3. When it comes to God, one of the most challenging questions is "who chooses whom?" In other words, does God choose us or do we choose him? For John Calvin, God knows all, is all powerful, and is sovereign over all, so it is not possible for us to choose him. Therefore, God chooses whom he will save and whom he will not. A young Francis de Sales was terrified by this proposition. How could he know if he was one of the elect? So, he did what any child would do … he ran to his mother! After praying the *Memorare* before a statue of the Blessed Mother, peace flooded his heart, and he never doubted the love of God again.

What is the lesson in this story for us about Mary's unique role in our lives?

_____
_____
_____

SESSION 6 - SAINT FRANCIS DE SALES

4. Saint Francis de Sales had a powerful experience when he celebrated the first Mass of his priesthood. He wrote: "In this first sacrifice, God took possession of my soul in an extraordinary way." Of course, in the backdrop, Calvinism had rejected the role of the ministerial priesthood. A central teaching of the Reformation was *Sola Christus*: salvation is accomplished by Christ alone and mediated by Christ alone—not by priests, sacraments, or anything else.

"By the mystery of this water and wine, may we come to share in the divinity of Christ, who humbled himself to share in our humanity." **How do these beautiful words proclaimed by the priest in the Mass encapsulate the difference between Catholicism and Protestantism?**

_____
_____
_____

5. Saint Francis de Sales won 30,000 Catholics back to full communion with the Church. He did so through his gentleness, courage, clear teaching, and innovative techniques, such as doctrinal tracts and religious education for children. He was serious when he told his brother priests as a young provost: "We are going to take back Geneva!"

Tragically, 1 in 10 Americans is a fallen away Catholic. In your opinion, what does the Church need to do to win them back?

_____
_____
_____
_____

6. The phrase "practice makes perfect" is an appropriate description for *Introduction to the Devout Life*. Jesus says to us: *"You, therefore, must be perfect, as your heavenly Father is perfect"* (Matthew 5:48). Devoted Catholics understand that we are always in the state of becoming. In other words, the combination of our own efforts and God's grace perfects us, though we are never fully actualized until we are united with God in Heaven.

By God's design, we participate in our own sanctification. Why do you think this is so, and what does sanctification have to do with salvation?

_____
_____
_____
_____

St. Francis de Sales, Sisak Cathedral, Croatia
© Zvonimir Atletic, Shutterstock.com

Commit

Saint Francis de Sales wrote a spiritual classic to help Catholics grow in sanctity: *The Introduction to the Devout Life*. The commitment this week is to read the first chapter of this classic, "What True Devotion Is."

"If I speak in the tongues of men and of angels, but have not love, I am a noisy gong or a clanging cymbal. And if I have prophetic powers, and understand all mysteries and all knowledge, and if I have all faith, so as to remove mountains, but have not love, I am nothing. If I give away all I have, and if I deliver my body to be burned, but have not love, I gain nothing."

—1 Corinthians 13:1–3

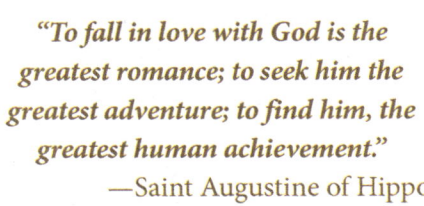

"To fall in love with God is the greatest romance; to seek him the greatest adventure; to find him, the greatest human achievement."
—Saint Augustine of Hippo

St. Francis de Sales, vintage engraved illustration
© Morphart Creation, Shutterstock.com

Closing Prayer

Do not look forward to the trials and crosses
of this life with dread and fear.
Rather, look to them with full confidence
that as they arise, God, to whom you belong,
will deliver you from them.

He has guided and guarded you
thus far in life.
Do you but hold fast to his dear hand, and
He will lead you safely through all trials.
Whenever you cannot stand,
he will carry you lovingly in his arms.

Do not look forward to what may happen tomorrow.
The same Eternal Father who cares for you today
will take good care of you tomorrow
and every day of your life.

Either he will shield you from suffering or
He will give you the unfailing strength to bear it.
Be at peace then and put aside all useless thoughts,
vain dreads, and anxious imaginations.

—Saint Francis de Sales
Saint Francis de Sales, pray for us.

SESSION 6 - SAINT FRANCIS DE SALES

EXCERPT FROM THE BOOK *TRUE REFORMERS*:

"Men accomplish more by love and charity than by severity and rigor." —Saint Francis de Sales

It can sometimes be forgotten that the most authentic work of the Church in any age, her most characteristic as well as her most impressive expression, is not to be sought in the books inspired by her teaching, or in the art and architecture and music she brings forth, or in the societies and organizations she founds, or in the political and social action she engenders. All these works, and many more besides, are among the genuine fruits of the Church's life. But more central than them all, and sustaining all the many outgrowths of the life of faith, is the Church's most profound expression: the formation of a distinctive human character. The various facets of the Church's life find their most complete integration in the human shape of those under her influence. Francis de Sales is an apt example of this kind of human and spiritual formation at work. He is the finest flower of the Catholic Reformation.

—Jerome K. Williams, *True Reformers* (Greenwood Village, Colorado: Augustine Institute, 2017), pp. 211–212.

NOTES

NOTES

TRUE REFORMERS
Suggested Answers for Group Leaders

Cover Images © Restored Traditions. Used with permission.

SESSION 1 – SAINT THOMAS MORE

1. How would you respond to someone who says that the Church will become more relevant in society if she de-emphasizes, or even changes those teachings that conflict with secular progressive values?

(Saint Toribio once said, "Christ said, 'I am the Truth'; he did not say 'I am the custom.'" Church teachings are not determined by the customs, ideologies, or trends of the day; they follow the truth that has been revealed by Jesus Christ and lead to him, who is Truth [cf. John 14:6], and this truth sets man free [cf. John 8:32]. In relating to one another, the Church must change the world, not the world change the Church (cf. James 4:4). The Church exists to evangelize, to speak the truth to the world—this is her "essential mission" [Evangelii Nuntiandi 14]. The Church exists in order to preach and teach the truth in the world, to guide the world into right living.)

2. How could you help an Evangelical Protestant understand the role of the saints in our lives when they believe that the Bible strictly forbids any form of communication with the dead?

(Catholics and Protestants alike pray for their family, friends, and others and ask others to pray for them as well. Asking for prayers is a biblical tradition; Saint Paul frequently asks for the intercessions of others in his letters [cf. Romans 15:30; 2 Corinthians 1:11; Philippians 1:19; Colossians 4:3]. Prayers to the saints are not acts of worship to them; they are prayers of intercession. Some Protestants may argue that the dead cannot hear our prayers, but in Revelation 5:8, Saint John depicts the saints in Heaven offering our prayers to God. This passage shows that the saints are aware of our prayers, meaning they can hear us. Some may argue that prayers to the saints are in vain since they are dead and cannot hear us. Jesus proclaimed that God is "not God of the dead, but of the living," and this same God is the God of Abraham, Isaac, and Jacob—all three who had died an earthly death [Matthew 22:32]. The saints and the deceased are still alive in the afterlife, and we enjoy communion with them: "'We believe in the communion of all the faithful of Christ, those who are pilgrims on earth, the dead who are being purified, and the blessed in heaven, all together forming one Church; and we believe that in this communion, the merciful love of God and his saints is always [attentive] to our prayers' [Paul VI, CPG § 30]" [CCC 962].)

3. If you were to develop a personal mission statement aimed at becoming the person God desires you to be, what would be your goals and your plan to achieve them?

(Answers will vary. One suggestion is growing in spiritual H.A.B.I.T.S., as discussed in other small group programs:

H – Holy Hour [commitment to daily, personal prayer]

A – Accountable Friendships [commitment to honest sharing and encouragement]

B – Bible [commitment to regularly reading, studying, and praying with Scripture]

I – Invest in Your Parish [commitment to tithing and serving in the parish]

T – Tell [commitment to share your faith in Jesus Christ with others]

S – Sacraments [commitment to frequent reception of Reconciliation and Eucharist]

We should all seek to grow in our personal vocations and strive to be the best spouse, father, mother, priest, or religious we can be.)

4. Why would Saint Thomas More consider Luther's teaching on human freedom and salvation "the very worst and most harmful heresy that was ever thought up"?

(If the human will and actions have no impact on man's salvation, then salvation relies entirely upon the decision of God, and God chooses who is saved and who is damned based off of nothing but his will. Luther's teaching leads to double predestination—the heavenly Father predestines some for Heaven and predestines some for Hell. The Bible tells us that in the plan of salvation, God is "not wishing that any should perish, but that all should reach repentance" [2 Peter 3:9]. God wills all souls to be saved, but individuals must choose to be united to God's will. Saint Augustine once said, "God created us without us: but he did not will to save us without us" [Sermo 169,11,13:PL 38,923], and the Catechism teaches that when God "establishes his eternal plan of 'predestination,' he includes in it each person's free response to his grace" [CCC 600]. Thinking that God chooses people for Hell undermines his goodness and man's free will. "In his infinite love, God sent his Son to die for our sins, and he offers each person the opportunity of salvation.")

5. With the Catholic Church's commitment to justice and the common good, why does the Church oppose those forms of socialism that seek to abolish the private ownership of property?

(The common good can be defined as "the sum total of social conditions which allow people, either as groups or as individuals, to reach their fulfillment more fully and more easily" [Gaudium et Spes 26]. Furthermore, the Catechism teaches that "the common good is always oriented towards the progress of persons" [CCC 1912]. Organizations, institutions, and societies all work in order to better the condition of the human person. Man does not participate in society in order to progress a specific ideology or system. Society as a whole ought to serve the human good of each individual. The furthering of human dignity is key to a well-functioning society: "a system that 'subordinates the basic rights of individuals and of groups to the collective organization of production' is contrary to human dignity" [CCC 2424]. The "public welfare" cannot infringe upon the dignity and rights of an individual. Economies and political orders are for the betterment of man, not vice versa. The socialism lived out in Utopia goes against the Catholic principle of subsidiarity, which "is opposed to all forms of collectivism. It sets limits for state intervention. It aims at harmonizing the relationships between individuals and societies. It tends toward the establishment of true international order" [CCC 1885]. By abolishing private goods, collectivist regimes undermine the integrity and freedom of individuals.)

Thomas More (1478-1535) © Georgios Kollidas, Shutterstock.com

6. A host of reputable studies demonstrate that a father is essential to the healthy development and total well-being of his children. And yet, from pop culture to the media, it would seem our nation places little value on the role of fathers. Why do you think this is the case and what can be done to empower fathers?

(Saint John Paul II wrote in Familiaris Consortio: *"The Christian family, in fact, is the first community called to announce the Gospel to the human person during growth and to bring him or her, through a progressive education and catechesis, to full human and Christian maturity"* [2]. *It is no wonder the family is under such attack. Satan knows he can destroy the family if he can remove the father from the family. As a counter-attack, the Church needs to help fathers understand the research on how significant their impact is on the healthy development of their children. Their presence, affection, affirmation, and leadership bring the security needed for children to thrive. On the other hand, a father's absence, either physically or emotionally, breeds insecurity. This is especially acute with adolescents. If fundamental emotional and psychological needs are not being met, teenagers are not motivated to meet higher growth needs like studying their Faith and committing their lives to it. Launching a men's movement in the parish that focuses on becoming better husbands and fathers is one way to empower fathers. Equipping fathers with resources to lead their families in faith formation in the home is another. Finally, small groups for men help them open up and receive support and encouragement. Men can bring the best out of one another as Proverbs 27:17 asserts: "Iron sharpens iron, and one man sharpens another."*)

Rome (Italy) - Saint Thomas More church in Villa Mercede
© ValerioMei, Shutterstock.com

Article - St. Charles Borromeo: Champion of Reform by Matthew Bunson

https://www.catholic.com/magazine/print-edition/champion-of-reform

For me, Charles Borromeo is the classic expression of a real reform, that is to say, of a renewal that leads forward precisely because it teaches how to live the permanent values in a new way, bearing in mind the totality of the Christian faith and the totality of man . . . he was totally centered on Christ... (The Ratzinger Report, page 38)

Charles could convince others because he himself was a man of conviction. He was able to exist with his certitudes amid the contradictions of his time because he lived them. And he could live them because he was a Christian in the deepest sense of the word; in other words, he was totally centered on Christ. What truly counts is to reestablish this all-embracing relation to Christ. No one can be convinced of this all-embracing relationship to Christ through argumentation alone. One can live it, however, and thereby make it credible to others and invite others to share it. (The Ratzinger Report, page 39)

A saint, reformer, cardinal, apologist, archbishop, and tireless pastor, St. Charles Borromeo rebuilt the Church in Milan during the 16th century and was one of the greatest figures of the Catholic Reformation. For Catholics laboring to renew the Church today in the face of a hostile culture, Borromeo stands as a champion of authentic renewal, as a gentle but determined saint, and as a powerful spokesman for the reinvigoration of the priesthood through zeal, commitment to the truth, and attracting solid, faithful seminarians. Above all, he is a reason for Catholics today to embrace the Catholic Reformation and the heroic men and women who led it.

Prayer

Do not look forward in fear to the changes in life;
rather, look to them with full hope that as they arise,
God, whose very own you are, will lead you safely through all
things; and when you cannot stand it, God will carry you in
His arms.

Do not fear what may happen tomorrow; the same
understanding Father who cares for you today will take care
of you then and every day.

He will either shield you from suffering or will give you
unfailing strength to bear it. Be at peace, and put aside all
anxious thoughts and imaginations.

—Saint Francis de Sales

SESSION 2 – SAINT IGNATIUS OF LOYOLA

1. The *Catechism of the Catholic Church* teaches that "prayer is a vital necessity" (2744) and even quotes Saint Alphonsus Liguouri, who wrote: "Those who pray are certainly saved; those who do not pray are certainly damned." In your view, why is prayer necessary for salvation, and how would you describe what this kind of prayer looks like?

(Reference Luke 18:10-14. The tax collector was justified because he recognized his spiritual poverty and called out to God. CCC 1847 quotes Saint Augustine: "God created us without us: but he did not will to save us without us." Like the tax collector, Saint Augustine was painfully aware of his sin and the only solution to that sin—the grace of God. This is why prayer is necessary for our salvation: We have to continually ask God for the grace of salvation and cooperate with that grace to conquer sin and death.)

2. The *Catechism* defines faith as "[entrusting] oneself wholly to God and [believing] absolutely what he says" [150]. In other words, faith involves a surrender of both our will and intellect. How do the saints show us what true faith is, and what prevents us from imitating them?

(Romans 12:2 reads: "Do not be conformed to this world but be transformed by the renewal of your mind, that you may prove what is the will of God, what is good and acceptable and perfect." The teachings of the Church are the teaching of Christ. We renew our minds by conforming our minds to the teachings of the Church. It is necessary to know the truth if we are to conform our lives to the truth with the aid of God's grace. A personal relationship with Jesus Christ, cultivated through prayer and the sacraments, motivates us to abandon ourselves more and more to Divine Providence.)

3. The Church teaches that Jesus Christ "fully reveals man to himself and makes his supreme calling clear" (*Gaudium et Spes*, 22). How do you think Jesus reveals to you a deeper understanding of yourself and your purpose in life?

(The Catechism *teaches that the Word became flesh: in order to save us by reconciling us with God; so we would know God's love; to be our model of holiness; and to make us partakers of the divine nature [457-460]. This means we are not the sum of our mistakes, are infinitely loved, can grow in selfless love, and have divine life dwelling within us. Our dignity is divine sonship and our mission is self-donation in imitation of Jesus Christ.)*

4. How would you respond to someone who says: "Catholics are guilty of idolatry in the way they regard Mary because the Bible nowhere instructs us to revere, pray to, or rely on anyone other than God"?

(The Catechism *teaches: "Mary's role in the Church is inseparable from her union with Christ and flows directly from it. 'This union of the mother with the Son in the work of salvation is made manifest from the time of Christ's virginal conception up to his death'; it is made manifest above all at the hour of his Passion" [964]. We imitate Christ when we honor Mary and enlist her help in God's plan of salvation.)*

5. To begin the "Spiritual Exercises," Saint Ignatius proposes a major consideration. How would you put that consideration into your own words?

(As the proverbial expression goes, "People don't plan to fail, they fail to plan"; so we should live with the end in mind. When we understand our ultimate end, we can order our decisions and actions to that end. In other words, our time on earth is meant to habituate us for eternal life in Heaven. Therefore, we need to be careful of developing attachments to this world, which is passing away. Jesus exhorts us: "Do not lay up for yourselves treasures on earth, where moth and rust consume and where thieves break in and steal, but lay up for yourselves treasures in heaven, where neither moth nor rust consumes and where thieves do not break in and steal. For where your treasure is, there will your heart be also" [Matthew 6:19-21].)

6. The movie/book poses a thought-provoking question: Would Jesus, in view of his mercy, want us to publicly renounce our faith in him that we might save ourselves, as well as others, from torture and death? How would you answer that question taking into consideration Saint Ignatius's "two standards"?

(This scene from the book/movie contradicts what Saint Paul writes to Timothy: "If we endure, we shall also reign with him; if we deny him, he also will deny us" [2 Timothy 2:12]. Of course, Jesus will forgive us of our sin when we sincerely repent. However, no matter how challenging the circumstances, we can be sure that Jesus will give us the grace to persevere. Saint Paul writes to the Corinthians: "God is faithful, and he will not let you be tempted beyond your strength, but with the temptation will also provide the way of escape, that you may be able to endure it" [1 Corinthians 10:13]. Finally, the Catechism *teaches: "Martyrdom is the supreme witness given to the truth of the faith: it means bearing witness even unto death. The martyr bears witness to Christ who died and rose, to whom he is united by charity. He bears witness to the truth of the faith and of Christian doctrine. He endures death through an act of fortitude" [2473].)*

Sanctuary of Loyola in Azpeitia, Basque Country
© Santi Rodriguez, Shutterstock.com

SESSION 3 – SAINT PHILIP NERI

1. What are we to make of this extraordinary experience and does it offer any illumination on the purpose and destiny of our bodies?

(The Catechism teaches: "In death, the separation of the soul from the body, the human body decays and the soul goes to meet God, while awaiting its reunion with its glorified body. God, in his almighty power, will definitively grant incorruptible life to our bodies by reuniting them with our souls, through the power of Jesus' Resurrection" [997]. We will be body and soul for all of eternity. Our glorified bodies will be physical, but will be different without the corruption of sin. In other words, they will be perfectly adapted to life in Heaven. Perhaps the story of Saint Philip Neri's heart and ribs demonstrate that our mortal bodies can't handle the unmitigated consuming fire of God's love, only a glorified body can.)

2. Saint Philip Neri wrote, "Our sweet Jesus, through the excess of his love and liberality, has left himself to us in the Most Holy Sacrament." And yet, approximately half of American Catholics are unaware of the Church's teaching on the Real Presence of Jesus in the Eucharist as the "source and summit of the Christian life" [CCC 1324]. In your opinion, why is this the case, and what be done to remedy the situation?

(Recent studies have shown that the overwhelming majority of Catholics do not pray or share their faith in the home. If the domestic Church is not alive in the faith, outside exposure to evangelization and catechesis has little to no impact. In other words, if parents do not understand and love the Real Presence of Jesus in the Eucharist, then neither will their children. More intentional evangelization and catechesis to parents is needed, especially to fathers. Studies also show that when fathers are engaged in the faith formation of their children, only a small percentage of their children abandon the Faith.)

3. How would you counsel a family member or friend who was determined to leave the Catholic Church because of moral failures within the leadership?

(The Church is one, holy, catholic, and apostolic. Without apostolic succession, we could not have the other three. Jesus entrusted authority to Peter and the Apostles, and they their successors. This was to safeguard the truth "that sets us free" [John 8:32]. We are united in the truth, we grow in holiness when our lives are conformed to the truth, and the Church is a universal (catholic) gift by proclaiming the truth to the nations. We trust in the office of authority Jesus established, regardless of the personal holiness of those who hold the office. In the absence of apostolic authority, chaos ensues, as the Protestant Reformation demonstrates. The relentless division within Protestantism has made truth relative and allowed for secularism to grow.)

4. Humility is not thinking less of yourself, but thinking of yourself less! What does this mean to you, and why is humility needed to acquire true peace and joy?

(Humility is central to Jesus teaching. For example, it is the "poor in spirit," "the meek," and "the merciful" who are blessed [Matthew 5:3–12]. The humble are blessed with peace and joy because they are free to love. On the contrary, those who are self-absorbed are not free to love. Fear and the inability to trust rob them of peace and joy. Tragically, the root cause is often neglect or abuse from childhood. Jesus, however, is the divine healer and can restore our view of ourselves in accordance with our dignity as beloved children of God.)

5. Why should we look to the Church for the correct interpretation of Scripture, and how would you articulate this to a "Bible only" Christian?

(The Bible is not sufficient in and of itself to resolve differing interpretations as the divisions within Protestantism prove. Sacred Scripture needs to be interpreted within context, and that context is provided in Sacred Tradition. Saint Paul writes to the Thessalonians: "So then, brethren, stand firm and hold to the traditions which you were taught by us, either by word of mouth or by letter" [2 Thessalonians 2:15]. Otherwise, individual interpretation of Scripture becomes nothing more than an autobiography. Truth was very important to Jesus. He says to Pilate: "For this I was born, and for this I have come into the world, to bear witness to the truth. Everyone who is of the truth hears my voice" [John 18:37]. Jesus established the teaching authority of the Church, the Magisterium, so that the Deposit of Faith would be safeguarded and handed down from generation to generation.)

6. We might think that the saints would have needed the Sacrament of Reconciliation less as they grew in sanctity. And yet, the opposite was the case. Why do you think that is?

(The Catechism *teaches: "The whole power of the sacrament of Penance consists in restoring us to God's grace and joining us with him in an intimate friendship" [1468]. The saints intimate friendship with God made them especially sensitive to their weaknesses, which impacted that friendship. Therefore, it was out of their great love for God that they went frequently to the Sacrament of Reconciliation. In other words, the process of purification creates a heightened awareness of impurities.)*

St Philip Neri and St Ignatius of Loyola Italian Baroque sculptures
© StockPhotosArt, Shutterstock.com

SESSION 4 – SAINT CHARLES BORROMEO

1. The True Reformers were obedient to the Church at a time when the authority of the Church was greatly challenged. Why is obedience a necessary virtue for Christian discipleship?

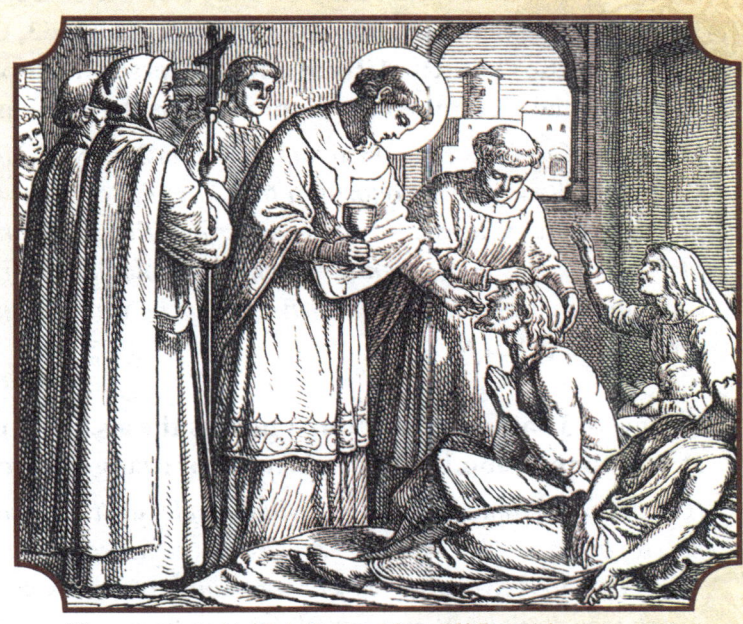

Old engravings. Depicts Saint Charles Borromeo © Sergey Kohl, Shutterstock.com

(*The* Catechism *teaches: "By faith, man completely submits his intellect and his will to God. With his whole being man gives his assent to God the revealer. Sacred Scripture calls this human response to God, the author of revelation, 'the obedience of faith'" [143]. The True Reformers understood what Blessed John Henry Newman would later write: "The most obvious answer to the question, why we yield to the authority of the Church in the questions and developments of faith, is that some authority there must be if a revelation is given, and other authority there is none but she" [The Development of Christian Doctrine, 88].*)

2. What did Saint Charles Borromeo understand that the rich young man in Matthew's Gospel did not?

(*Saint Charles Borromeo had so profoundly encountered the love of Christ that he desired intimacy with him above everything else. He knew how unsatisfying possessions were in comparison to union with Jesus. In Matthew 6, Jesus says: "No one can serve two masters; for either he will hate the one and love the other, or he will be devoted to the one and despise the other. You cannot serve God and mammon" [v. 24]. Then Jesus invites us to place our faith in him for all our provisions: "Therefore I tell you, do not be anxious about your life, what you shall eat or what you shall drink, nor about your body, what you shall put on" [v.25]. We are tempted to trust in our own resources, and not in Christ. The more resources, the greater that challenge can be, as the rich young man demonstrates.*)

3. What does the crucifix tell us about the meaning and purpose of our lives?

(*Jesus's complete gift of himself in love on the Cross gave us a window into the inner life of the Trinity. This is the kind of love shared within the life of God. Jesus calls us to this kind of love and makes it possible by giving us grace that flows from his Paschal Mystery—his life, Death, and Resurrection. As we gaze upon the crucifix, we are reminded that we are infinitely loved and the purpose of our lives is to be given away in love. As Saint Paul writes to the Galatians: "I have been crucified with Christ; it is no longer I who live, but Christ who lives in me; and the life I now live in the flesh I live by faith in the Son of God, who loved me and gave himself for me" [2:20].*)

4. In 1559 Angelo Medici, the uncle of Saint Charles Borromeo, was elected pope and took the name of Pius IV. He made Charles Borromeo a cardinal and secretary of state between 1560 and 1567. Ordained to the priesthood in 1563, Charles was asked by the pope to preside at the Council of Trent and to oversee its implementation. In your estimation, why was Cardinal Borromeo the right man for these times?

(To begin, Cardinal Borromeo had moral authority. A man who had reformed his own life had the credibility to call for reform in the Church. Secondly, Cardinal Borromeo's detachment from personal gain, be it wealth, status, or recognition, made him an influential leader at the Council of Trent. He was instrumental in helping theologians work through differences in doctrine and in keeping the council fathers unified. Finally, he was exemplary in implementing the reforms that the Council called for.)

5. How did Saint Charles Borromeo, as the archbishop of the largest diocese in the world at that time, embody these principles of evangelization and catechesis?

(Cardinal Borromeo understood that people don't care how much you know until they know how much you care. Therefore, he traveled to the far corners of his diocese to teach doctrine and to call people to conversion. He was insistent on reforms and modeled them in his own household, which was disciplined and frugal. His efforts were met with much resistance, but he pressed on. He cared for people in establishing orphanages, hospitals, and seminaries. The principles of evangelization and catechesis he embodied were authentic witness, relational approach, pastoral care, bold teaching, and indomitability.)

6. In a nationwide study of college students done at the University of Texas, over one-half admitted to having thoughts of taking their own lives. Charles Borromeo understood from a very young age that his life was not his own. How can we help young people today understand that their lives are not their own?

(Many years ago, renowned psychologist Erik Erikson—best known for coining the phrase "identity crisis"—released conclusions from his studies about the problem of purposelessness and its consequences in young adults. He determined that self-absorption, depression, and a variety of emotionally related physical ailments are often the result of not having a motivating belief system that gives a sense of purpose to life. Parents have the greatest influence in handing the Faith onto their children. The home should be a place of prayer and faith sharing. In addition, teenagers need parents and other caring adults who will be present and willing to dialogue with them about issues of faith and life. Otherwise, they can be easily led astray by the moral relativism in the culture.)

View of St. Charles's Church in Vienna, Austria © Minoli, Shutterstock.com

SESSION 5 – SAINT TERESA OF ÁVILA

1. Saint Teresa of Ávila wrote in Interior Castle: "It is foolish to think that we will enter Heaven without entering into ourselves." What do you think that she meant by this profound statement, and how does it relate to the danger of cultural Catholicism?

(Saint Teresa was speaking from experience. When she was in a state of poor health, she ceased her daily habit of mental prayer. Consequently, she became more attracted to worldly things. The interior life habituates us for life in Heaven, where we will see God, love him, and be united to him in an indissoluble embrace. Mental prayer is "entering into ourselves" to meet God and grow in intimacy with him. It helps us to remove the distractions of a world that is passing away. There is a saying: "Rules without relationship results in rebellion." Without an interior life, Catholicism becomes rules without relationship.)

Saint Theresa of Ávila sculpture at the "Plaza del Grande" © Blazar SLU, Shutterstock.com

2. How does this parable of the lonely ember relate to the decisions Sister Teresa made to reform religious life?

(Sister Teresa removed herself from the worldly distractions occurring at the monastery—like the social visits with the public in the parlor, the constant chatter in the community, and the recreation times. She began spending time outside the monastery at a friend's where she grew in prayer, spiritual reading, and fellowship. She was convinced that the laxity in Incarnation was due to having too many nuns. So, in her new community she limited the number of nuns to just thirteen, who were strictly cloistered, and barely spoke to one another. She had created a community, committed to prayer and mortifications, that helped them grow brightly in the fire of God's love.)

3. Pope Saint John Paul II, in his Apostolic Letter *At the Beginning of the Third Millennium*, writes of a "renewed need for prayer" [33] and points us to the "great mystical tradition of the Church" as evidence of how prayer can progress. In your opinion, how is a lay person to interpret his exhortation?

(Karol Wojtyla, as a young man, was profoundly impacted by a gentleman named Jan Tyranowski. A tailor by trade, Tyranowski had developed an extraordinary prayer life inspired by the writings of Saint Teresa of Ávila and Saint John of the Cross. He introduced Karol to the writings of these great saints and helped him develop a prayer life of his own. Pope John Paul II would later write about Tyranowski: "His way of life proved that one could not only inquire about God but that one could live with God" [Witness to Hope 61]. We are all called to "live with God." The Catechism teaches: "Christian prayer is a covenant relationship between God and man in Christ" [2564]. The mystical tradition of the Church gives us the confidence of just how much we can grow in our covenant relationship with God.)

4. First John 4:18 reads: "There is no fear in love, but perfect love casts out fear." What do you think is the practical application of this verse to our lives?

(In the Letter to the Hebrews, we read: "Since therefore the children share in flesh and blood, he himself likewise partook of the same nature, that through death he might destroy him who has the power of death, that is, the devil, and deliver all those who through fear of death were subject to lifelong bondage" [2:14-15]. In other words, fear is from the enemy and it has the power to enslave us because of our sinful nature. The root cause of fear is the wounds we experience from our own sin and the sins of others. Jesus's perfect love can heal our wounds and deliver us from our fears. Trust in Jesus is the antidote. He will deliver us from our fears, giving us the freedom to love ourselves and others.)

5. If someone were to say to you: "Why pray for the intercession of Saint Joseph when you can pray directly to Jesus? Why complicate the matter with a middle man?"

(The Catechism *teaches that the saints in Heaven "contemplate God, praise him and constantly care for those whom they have left on earth. When they entered into the joy of their Master, they were 'put in charge of many things.' Their intercession is their most exalted service to God's plan. We can and should ask them to intercede for us and for the whole world" [2683]. In other words, God wants us to ask for the intercession of the saints and the saints want to intercede for us! When we pray to Saint Joseph and the saints, we know that whatever graces and favors we receive come to us from God, through their intercession. If we value the prayers of our friends on earth and feel that those prayers will help us, the prayers of our friends in Heaven will be even more powerful, for as Saint Thomas Aquinas says, "The more closely one is united to God, the more efficacious will be his/her prayers." As the Patron Saint of the Universal Church, Saint Joseph's paternal protection of the Lord Jesus continues even from Heaven, as he watches over Christ's Mystical Body on earth.)*

6. What principles of effective leadership can be drawn out from this story of Saint Teresa?

(Leadership experts Ken Blanchard and Phil Hodges wrote a book titled "Lead Like Jesus." As the title suggests, they point to Jesus as the perfect leadership role model. Jesus's motivations were selfless, always submitting himself to the will of his Father. His vision was servant leadership, dedicating himself to the betterment of others. And, he had the habit of recharging himself through frequent solitude and prayer so that he could be strengthened in his service to others. Saint Teresa of Ávila was likewise selfless in her motivations, dedicated to the reform of woman religious starting with those sisters closest to her, and was committed to solitude and prayer as the source of the strength she could offer to those she led.)

Convent of Santa Teresa in Ávila (Spain) © danileon, Shutterstock.com

SESSION 6 - SAINT FRANCIS DE SALES

1. John Calvin argued that we cannot come to know God through created things but only through Scripture. What is the Catholic position on this matter?

(Ironically, Calvin's thought contradicts Saint Paul's letter to the Romans: "Ever since the creation of the world his invisible nature, namely, his eternal power and deity, has been clearly perceived in the things that have been made" [1:20]. Faith is our response to God's revelation, the fullness of which is in the Person of Jesus Christ. However, God also gifted us with reason to observe the world around us and come to truths about reality. Saint John Paul II wrote an encyclical titled "Faith and Reason," and he affirms the Catholic position in the first sentence: "Faith and reason are like two wings on which the human spirit rises to the contemplation of truth." In other words, the absence of faith or reason will diminish our ability to know ourselves, the world, and God.)

2. Jesus's high priestly prayer in John chapter 17 is for unity among his followers: "Holy Father, keep them in thy name, which thou hast given me, that they may be one, even as we are one" (v.11). In what ways is Saint Francis de Sales a model for us as someone who worked for and achieved unity in a time of painful division?

(Saint Francis de Sales would likely not agree with the statement: "You should never talk about religion or politics." He understood that if we don't talk about matters that cause conflict and division, we rob ourselves of the opportunity to grow and reconcile. Known for his patience and gentleness, Saint Francis would speak the truth in love. In the beginning, he was rejected. But he persevered, writing out his homilies and sliding them under the doors of homes, printing out Catholic tracts, catechizing children and winning back their parents, and boldly living the Catholic Faith. Saint Francis de Sales brought some 40,000–50,000 Catholics back into full communion with the Church. Courage, patience, gentleness, and perseverance are needed to facilitate reconciliation and restore unity.)

3. What is the lesson in this story for us about Mary's unique role in our lives?

(The Catechism *teaches: "Scripture portrays the tragic consequences of this first disobedience. Adam and Eve immediately lose the grace of original holiness. They become afraid of the God of whom they have conceived a distorted image—that of a God jealous of his prerogatives" [399]. In other words, our view of our heavenly Father is distorted, we fear him, and we fail to trust. Mary, on the other hand, completely entrusted herself to the Father's plan of salvation. "By her obedience, she became the new Eve, mother of the living" [CCC 511]. As our mother, Mary can help us to overcome our fear and see ourselves as our heavenly Father considers us, as his beloved children.)*

The metropolitan cathedral Saint Francis de Sales in Chambery © Fabio Lotti, Shutterstock.com

4. "By the mystery of this water and wine, may we come to share in the divinity of Christ, who humbled himself to share in our humanity." How do these beautiful words proclaimed by the priest in the Mass encapsulate the difference between Catholicism and Protestantism?

(The Catechism *teaches: "The Word became flesh to make us 'partakers of the divine nature'" [460]. In other words, Jesus has made it possible for the Holy Trinity to live within us. This is sanctifying grace, a share in divine life, that we receive in the sacraments, most especially in the Eucharist in which is "the body and blood, together with the soul and divinity, of our Lord Jesus Christ" [CCC 1374]. Protestants do not share our belief in sanctifying grace, the sacraments, the Real Presence of Jesus, and how divine life is dispensed through the Church.)*

St. Francis de Sales, vintage engraved illustration
© Morphart Creation, Shutterstock.com

5. Tragically, 1 in 10 Americans is a fallen away Catholic. In your opinion, what does the Church need to do to win them back?

(The majority of those who have left the Catholic Church, when surveyed, point to "family tension" as the primary reason for leaving. If this is the case, then what is needed most of all is reconciliation within families. Parents who reach out to their children and apologize for ways they have hurt them or failed to hand on to them a life-giving faith, create the greatest possibility of their return. In addition, any outreach to fallen away Catholics is a ministry of reconciliation. Humility, empathic listening, pastoral dialogue, and saying "I'm sorry" is needed because we are dealing with someone who is estranged from the family, the Body of Christ, whether they are aware of that or not. Finally, the more Catholics understand the biblical and theological foundations for their faith, the greater their ability to speak the truth in love. Getting as many people as possible in the parish to study their faith should be the priority of the pastor and his lay leaders.)

6. By God's design, we participate in our own sanctification. Why do you think this is so, and what does sanctification have to do with salvation?

(Saint Paul writes to the Corinthians: "And we all, with unveiled face, beholding the glory of the Lord, are being changed into his likeness from one degree of glory to another; for this comes from the Lord who is the Spirit" [3:18]. This is the process of sanctification—to be changed into the likeness of Jesus Christ by the power of the Holy Spirit. Jesus "emptied himself, taking the form of a servant, being born in the likeness of men. And being found in human form he humbled himself and became obedient unto death, even death on a cross" [Philippians 2:7-8]. The Holy Spirit will help us to "empty ourselves" but our cooperation is necessary. If we are to become like Jesus, we must have the power to submit or reject God's will in our lives.)

TAKING CATHOLIC BIBLE STUDY TO A NEW LEVEL

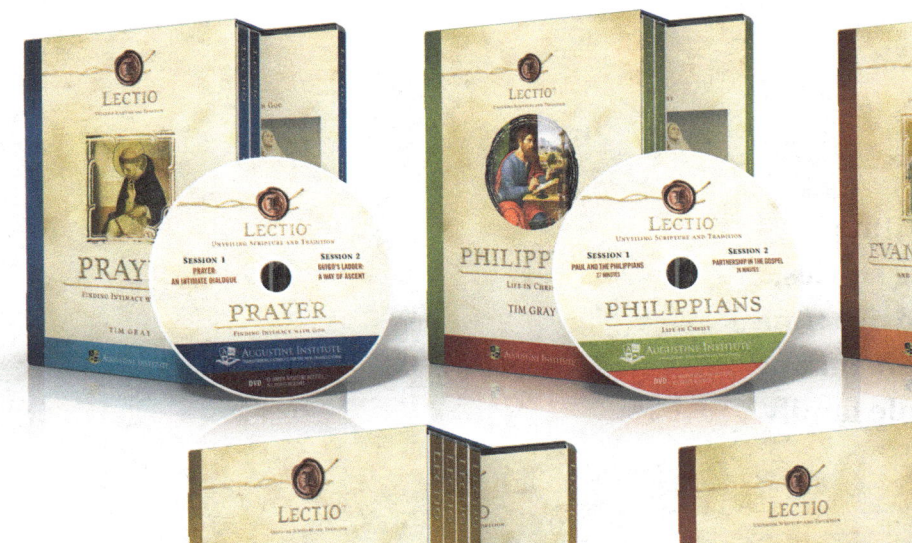

Compelling Catholic presenters bring together insightful teaching and practical guidance to make Scripture come alive.

AugustineInstitute.org/lectio

Stories and Saints
As You've Never Heard Them Before

With Augustine Institute Radio Theatre's inspiring stories, meal time, bedtime, and drive time can be a time for entertainment and faith-building for the whole family.

Brother Francis:
The Barefoot Saint of Assisi
(BFRANC-D) $29.95
5-CD Set

The Trials of Saint Patrick
(TSPAT-D) $29.95
4-CD Set

AUGUSTINE INSTITUTE®
RADIO THEATRE

Learn more at airtheatre.org